Pollution
Prevention
Economics

Other McGraw-Hill Environmental Engineering Books of Interest

AMERICAN WATER WORKS ASSOCIATION • *Water Quality and Treatment*

BAKER • *Bioremediation*

BRUNNER • *Hazardous Waste Incineration, 2d ed.*

CALLAHAN, GREEN • *Hazardous Solvent Source Reduction*

CASCIO, WOODSIDE, MITCHELL • *ISO 14000*

CHOPEY • *Environmental Engineering in the Process Plant*

COOKSON • *Bioremediation Engineering: Design and Application*

CORBITT • *Standard Handbook of Environmental Engineering*

CURRAN • *Environmental Life Cycle Assessment*

FREEMAN • *Hazardous Waste Minimization*

FREEMAN • *Industrial Pollution Prevention Handbook*

FREEMAN • *Standard Handbook of Hazardous Waste Treatment and Disposal*

HARRIS, HARVEY • *Hazardous Chemicals and the Right to Know*

HAYS, GOBBELL, GANICK • *Indoor Air Quality: Solutions and Strategies*

JAIN • *Environmental Impact Assessment*

KOLLURU • *Environmental Strategies Handbook*

KOLLURU • *Risk Assessment and Management Handbook*

KRIETH • *Handbook of Solid Waste Management*

LEVIN, GEALT • *Biotreatment of Industrial and Hazardous Waste*

LUND • *The McGraw-Hill Recycling Handbook*

MAJUMDAR • *Regulatory Requirements of Hazardous Materials*

McKENNA & CUNNEO • *Pesticide Regulation Handbook*

ROSSITER • *Waste Minimization through Process Design*

SELDNER, COETHRAL • *Environmental Decision Making for Engineering and Business Managers*

SMALLWOOD • *Solvent Recovery Handbook*

WALDO, HINES • *Chemical Hazard Communications Guidebook*

WILLIG • *Environmental TQM*

Pollution Prevention Economics

Financial Impacts on Business and Industry

James R. Aldrich, Ph.D.

McGraw-Hill

New York   San Francisco   Washington, D.C.   Auckland   Bogotá
Caracas   Lisbon   London   Madrid   Mexico City   Milan
Montreal   New Delhi   San Juan   Singapore
Sydney   Tokyo   Toronto

Library of Congress Cataloging-in-Publication Data

Aldrich, James R.
   Pollution prevention economics : financial impacts on business and
industry / James R. Aldrich.
       p.   cm.
   Includes bibliographical references and index.
   ISBN 0-07-000993-7
   1. Pollution—Economic aspects.   2. Environmental auditing.
3. Environmental policy.   4. Environmental law—Compliance costs.
I. Title.
HC79.P55A38   1996
658.15'53—dc20

95-46151
CIP

McGraw-Hill

A Division of The McGraw-Hill Companies

1 2 3 4 5 6 7 8 9 0   DOC/DOC   9 0 0 9 8 7 6 5

ISBN 0-07-000993-7

*The sponsoring editor for this book was Zoe G. Foundotos, the editing supervisor was
Stephen M. Smith, and the production supervisor was Pamela A. Pelton. It was set
in Palatino by Victoria Khavkina of McGraw-Hill's Professional Book Group composi-
tion unit.*

Printed and bound by R. R. Donnelley & Sons Company.

McGraw-Hill books are available at special quantity discounts to use as premiums and sales promotions, or for use in corporate training programs. For more
information, please write to the Director of Special Sales, McGraw-Hill, 11
West 19th Street, New York, NY 10011. Or contact your local bookstore.

This book is printed on recycled, acid-free paper containing a
minimum of 50% recycled de-inked fiber.

Contents

Foreword

The Environmental Protection Agency (EPA) was instituted in 1970 as a regulatory agency "to address and clean up" environmental problems. Since that time EPA has developed a myriad of environmental regulations, most of which employ the strategy of treating and/or controlling pollution after it is generated. Application of this strategy has led to the development of a culture in the United States that says that it is perfectly acceptable to generate pollutants as long as society can control their effects on humans and the environment.

Generally, the average citizen has developed a culture that ignores or tolerates environmental pollution until some major or drastic environmental event or circumstance occurs, at which time overreaction is often the chosen course of action. At the same time, industry has developed a culture, driven by environmental laws, rules, and regulations, that emphasizes the control of pollution after production through the application of control equipment or waste treatment technology to reduce health or environmental risks. As a result of the legal and economic effects often imposed by environmental laws, a spirit of protectionism often exists in an industry, and antagonism can quickly develop between industry, the public, and governmental agencies. Meanwhile, the legislatures of both state and federal governments seem to be perpetuating the "end-of-pipe control" culture in recently passed legislation. All this continues to result in regulations which simply transfer pollutants from one medium to another, not the eradication of pollutants.

With the passage of the Pollution Prevention Act of 1990, the first real opportunity to change the pollutant production culture that has developed in the United States over the past 25 years has been presented. As defined in the Act, pollution prevention means, basically, "source reduction" and other practices that *reduce or eliminate the creation of pollutants*. The Act creates a pollution prevention hierarchy which specifically states that disposal or release of pollution into the environment should be employed only as a last resort and then only in an environmentally safe manner.

Pollution prevention has been accepted by both environmentalists and the regulated industrial community. Environmentalists accept the culture of pollution prevention because it reduces pollution at the source before it enters the environment. The main problem in changing their culture will be their accepting pollution prevention regulations in place of end-of-pipe treatment regulations, which may be difficult to measure or monitor even though they have the potential to be greatly more beneficial to human health and the environment. The incentive for industry is money. Certainly, industrial processes can be made more profitable when pollutant control, disposal, and liability costs are minimized through a pollution prevention program.

This book enables the reader to understand the process of how to obtain funds for pollution prevention projects. In doing so, it stresses the applying of pollution prevention programs to the economic evaluation of either new or existing industrial processes. Because this book recognizes that engineers are not economists and vice versa, it bridges the gap between environmental engineering and the economic concerns of these processes. The author addresses microeconomics, engineering economics, accounting principles, and pollution prevention mechanics in such a manner as to be understandable and useful to engineers, business personnel, and management personnel.

The ultimte use of this book is in presenting information to gain capital investment for pollution prevention activities which when implemented will generate a body of data and information that will document the efficacy of pollution prevention as a concept. Stated another way, money will be required to implement pollution prevention programs which may effect the desired culture change with respect to environmental pollution. As long as pollution prevention is subservient to economic, legal, political, and social concerns, it will not take its place in the hierarchy of environmentalism. This book presents information that will assist in adopting an environmental pollution prevention culture as we enter the twenty-first century.

Thomas R. Hauser, Ph.D.
Research Professor, College of Engineering, University of Cincinnati
and Past Executive Director of the
American Institute for Pollution Prevention

Preface

Engineers are confronted with two impor-
tant interconnected environments, the phys-
ical and the economic. Their success . . .
depends upon a knowledge of physical laws.
However, the worth of these products and
services lies in their utility measured in
economic terms. There are numerous
examples of structures, machines, processes
and systems that exhibit excellent physical
design, but have little economic merit.
WALTER J. FRABRYCKY AND GERALD J. THUESEN
Engineering Economy, 5th ed.,
Prentice-Hall, 1977

The field of environmental management is beginning to take on
the prominence that was once the sole domain of environmental
engineering. Although the technical issues involved in controlling emissions, the fate and transport of pollutants, and so on
have by no means diminished in importance, the business world
is painfully aware that these actions must be paid for within a
business's investment scheme. These often costly issues require
the investment of a large amount of a business's profits, and,

because the "well" has been visited so often, the environmental sections within a firm are often seen as black holes or perfect cost sinks which do little more than take profits away from other investment opportunities. It is the responsibility of the environmental manager to dispel this notion and to show how environmental requirements, if correctly analyzed and presented, actually represent investment opportunities.

Hence, this text emphasizes obtaining investment capital for pollution prevention. Whether from banks, from investors, or from a controlling committee within a business or corporation, pollution prevention investment must be able to compete with other projects and investment opportunities within a firm. The text sections—economics, accounting, engineering economics, and so on—all support this one underlying theme: obtaining resources to support investment in pollution prevention.

Although this overwhelming emphasis on the financial and investment aspects might seem to oversimplify the impact that pollution prevention can have in addressing many of the environmental "problems," bringing together both the technical and financial components is critical. In the past, environmental issues have typically been seen as a confrontation between those who desire a "clean" environment and those that are required to make a profit in order to remain in business. However, an analysis of pollution prevention investment can show that these two goals are not mutually exclusive. If a pollution prevention project can be shown to be profitable, the confrontation ends; if pollution is eliminated, those desiring a cleaner environment succeed; if the project is profitable, those who need profit to survive in the business likewise succeed; and, as an unplanned benefit, less cost to the supplier implies that consumers in general will see lower prices. Emphasizing economics and profitability rather than the purely technical aspects of pollution prevention is critical to changing this traditional battlefield into a true win-win-win situation.

This book has been designed to benefit business at any level. It will give small business owners and operators the tools they need to examine the profitability of a pollution prevention investment within their firms. They will gain either the expertise to make decisions regarding the allocation of their own resources or the facts which will allow them to seek loans and/or investment from outside their firms. Similarly, person-nel in large firms, corporations, government agencies, and the like, where investment must be approved by a governing board, can benefit because they too will have the skills to show the profitability of their pollution prevention investment opportuni-ties.

In addition to being a professional text, this book may be used in its current form to support an undergraduate college-level course which combines the three disciplines of microeconomics, engineering economics, and accounting. It could similarly be used at the graduate level with the inclusion of a major design project or paper required by the instructor.

Given the breadth of coverage, this text cannot deal with the intricacies of each topic in great detail but does serve well as a management guide to computing the financial impact of capital investment in pollution prevention. Further, the reader can gain a firm understanding of the interrelationship of pollution pre-vention and profit. This basic knowledge is critical to placing the management of a pollution prevention program in correct context so that expenses and benefits can be recognized and accounted for properly. With the ability to compute accurately financial impacts, pollution prevention investment shall be able to stand up to other corporate investment alternatives and receive the resources deserved and required.

This text is arranged from the abstract, the theory behind pol-lution prevention investment, to the specific, the actual nuts and bolts of computing the net present value of pollution prevention alternatives. By developing the underlying theory as well as the tools, this book will help readers not only to produce a dollar figure representing the net present value of a pollution preven-tion investment, but, more important, to develop an under-standing of both how the analysis is performed and the inherent uncertainties in such calculations, an understanding which "cookbook" approaches cannot provide.

Throughout the text, the mathematics used in developing the theory and in applying the tools has been simplified to the max-imum extent possible. Admittedly, mathematical simplification can and does induce error into the analysis; however, this error is of little consequence to the usefulness of the analysis within the financial decision process as presented herein. This is because there is no such thing as the perfect financial analysis. Investment analysis requires the prediction of future events such as price increases and/or decreases and discount rates, variables which can either increase or decrease freely and frequently. Alternatively, the inaccuracy caused by the mathematical simplifications can be predicted and accounted for in the analysis or in the presentation of results. More important, these simplifications make the text understandable to a great many more readers. Those with only basic skills in algebra will have no problem in both understanding and using this text.

Section 1, "Microeconomics," begins with an examination of the theory under which all businesses operate in a free-market economy, supply and demand. From there, the concepts of consumer surplus, marginal costs and benefits, externalities, and optimization are introduced with numerous examples explaining how a firm can use this information to optimize its profits. Finally, as is the case with all the sections, a list of study concepts is provided. To either the manager or the student, these concepts can serve as a measure or metric of how well the information presented in the section is understood.

As Sec. 1 provided the theory, Sec. 2, "Engineering Economics," provides the tools needed to examine any potential investment with specific emphasis on pollution prevention. Both benefit-cost analysis and present value analyses of expenses and revenues are covered. In addition, the common selection methods used in the investment decision process, such as payback period and rate of return, are presented and examined from the standpoint of their applicability and limitations in analyzing pollution prevention investment opportunities.

Section 3, "Accounting Principles," examines the language of business. The concepts presented and discussed include cash flow and benefit and cost analysis, and a special emphasis is given to categorizing the revenues and expenses developed in Sec. 2 into standard accounting classifications. This section is not a full treatise on accounting and should not be used as a substitute for standard accounting methods. Its presentation is part of the complete package of understanding pollution prevention investment and serves to introduce environmental management personnel to the language of business.

Section 4, "The Mechanics of Establishing Pollution Prevention Alternatives," provides a synopsis of pollution prevention legislation, pollution prevention opportunity surveys, and measurement. Emphasis is given to the prediction of waste from input data such as production predictions and input materials. In addition, a case study examining the long-term liability of landfilling hazardous waste is included as an appendix to illustrate the concepts shown in text.

Section 5, "Some Last Thoughts," provides a summary of the role pollution prevention has played and will play with respect to investment.

James R. Aldrich, Ph.D.

Acknowledgments

This work is dedicated to my wife Caroline and my sons Cory and Jeremy, who spent long hours listening to the "tick tick tick" of the keyboard and reading draft manuscripts. They understood why I felt I had to write this book, and for their patience I am forever grateful.

In addition, I would like to thank the American Institute for Pollution Prevention, Dr. Thomas Hauser, (Past) Executive Director; and the Environmental Protection Agency, Dr. David Stephan, Pollution Prevention Research Branch, Risk Reduction Engineering Laboratory, for their support of my writing a predecessor of this text, *A Primer for Financial Analysis of Pollution Prevention Projects*, EPA/600/R-93/059, April 1993, one of the most requested publications ever! If it wasn't for their foresight in seeing the need for environmental management to take a place next to the traditional engineering fields, the present book may have never been written.

Finally, I would like to thank Dr. Charles A. Berry, University of Cincinnati, and Mr. Elliott Berkihiser for their support and review of this text and their help in making it a more useful treatise. To Dr. Berry, a special thanks for hooking me on economics and helping me form the marriage between the engineering and managerial fields.

Introduction

There is a growing knowledge gap in environmental management. On one side stands the scientist or engineer with technological expertise and on the other, the manager who knows how
to make a profit. This gap surfaced as the need for advanced
technical expertise forced the change from sanitary to environmental engineering.

Historically, sanitary engineering was the province of the civil
engineer. However, as our knowledge of the interactions and
complexities of the environment developed, the field has grown
beyond a subspecialty. The increased technical expertise
required, first manifested by the addition of new fields such as
ecology, has led to basic changes in the field. Colleges and uni-
versities responded by developing specialized engineering curriculum, and there has been an increase in the number of persons from pure scientific backgrounds entering the field. The
influx of expertise has led to quantum leaps in understanding
the environmental problems facing society today; however, this
knowledge did not come without cost.

Historically, the "sanitary" engineer's basic undergraduate
curriculum was relatively constant with all graduates taking
core courses in microeconomics, accounting, and engineering
economics. Conversely, the graduates from the various scientific

disciplines who were joining the environmental field often lacked such courses. Although the scientific curricula had their own set of core courses, their discipline often neither required nor allowed for these basic undergraduate economics courses. This problem or "academic blind spot" has been further exacerbated—as the need for specialized, technically advanced undergraduate courses grew, traditional core courses often had to be either eliminated or abbreviated. As a result, one can no longer assume that graduates tasked with environmental management have had courses in accounting, microeconomics, and/or engineering economics. In addition, given the growth of environmental regulations, environmental management personnel frequently come from nonscientific, nonengineering backgrounds. This is especially true for small business entrepreneurs who have had the environmental management role thrust upon them.

The development of such technical specialization has led to the knowledge barrier between those involved in the technical and the managerial issues faced in the business of environmental management. Management personnel understand the business of pollution prevention but not the technical aspects. Similarly, the environmental engineers and scientists understand the technical aspects but have not had exposure to financial analysis of investment alternatives. Simply put, the scientists know what needs to be done but do not have the expertise to present their requirements on a business level.

This text was prepared to provide a bridge across that information gap. Most important, it was designed to serve the technical community by providing the basic economic and accounting skills required to financially justify pollution prevention investment opportunities. Second, this text can further serve to illustrate to the financial community that environmental requirements and pollution prevention investment can be used to impact a company or firm's "bottom line." Only through an understanding of the interrelationship of these two critical areas will it be possible to take full advantage of investment opportunities in pollution prevention.

1
Microeconomics

Microeconomics is at the heart of the free market system and is based on the supply and demand for goods and services within a market. A basic understanding of how prices are related to these supply and demand functions will shed light on a variety of financial questions such as these: What will be the effect on the amount of goods sold given a specific change in price? How do price ceilings and floors affect the equilibrium market situation? How much should be charged for a particular item? Some of these questions may seem either elementary or beyond the control of a supplier. For example, if the market price of a ballpoint pen is $0.49, an individual supplier can do little about it. However, understanding how the price of the pen was set at $0.49 instead of $4.90 is critical. An understanding of how the supply and demand relationships work with price within the market is critical to properly justifying pollution prevention investment.

In establishing and understanding the basic supply and demand relationship the concepts of consumer surplus, marginal cost and benefit, and externalities will also be examined. Then these concepts will be applied in environmental management situations to illustrate how these basic tenets can be used to enable the reader to answer questions such as the following: What price should be paid for an air permit? What level of investment in pollution prevention equipment is economically sound? What are the pros and cons of the three major permitting systems either used or proposed in emission management today: command and control, fees, and marketable permits? By understanding the fundamentals, the analyses that can be performed are as endless as the number of applications in environmental management.

Supply and Demand

Price determination through the supply and demand relationships forms the basis of microeconomics. Although the market and in turn the relationship between these variables is dynamic, analysis is not impossible or even difficult. By confining the study to the market conditions at a single point in time, the normally dynamic supply and demand functions can be represented graphically. Freezing the functions in this manner allows us to draw the distinction between the demand function which represents the demand for a good (D) and the quantity demanded (Q_d) as well as between the supply function which represents the supply of a good (S) and the quantity supplied (Q_s). The difference between the two quantities (e.g., the demand for a good versus quantity of the good demanded) is determined by price, and it is price, or changes in price, that is critical in microeconomic analysis. Because the analysis is necessarily limited to a snapshot in time, the supply and demand functions become fixed, making price the only independent variable in the market. More important, as the only independent variable, price is the only variable which affects the five functions of an economic system. Under the free market system, given a competitive market, the independent variable, price, will determine:

- The type and quantity of goods provided—if there is demand, demonstrated by the consumer's willingness to pay, the goods shall be supplied
- The minimal cost method of production for the good—suppliers will act to maximize profit
- The distribution of the goods—suppliers will act to ensure sufficient supply to consumers willing to purchase same

- The rationing of the goods via speculation and futures markets—suppliers will act in response to expected changes in the market
- The provision for growth (savings)—suppliers will build equity in their firms

Because price is the only independent variable in the analysis, and it can affect all the functions of the market system, it can be used to predict both the quantity supplied and quantity demanded within a market.

Conversely, in such an analysis, the supply and demand functions for any individual good become dependent variables, and these functions are governed by empirical laws and parameters. The *law of demand* states that consumers are willing to buy more of any given good at lower prices than at higher prices given constant demand parameters. These parameters and their effect on consumers' decisions to purchase goods are as follows:

- *Consumer income.* Consumers' buying habits change with changes in income; nearly everyone has experienced the joy of "splurging" after receiving an increase in salary or an income tax refund.
- *Tastes and preferences.* Consumers' demand is often faddish, which affects their buying habits. For example, recall how the demand rose and fell for faddish items such as Nehru jackets, hula hoops, and pet rocks.
- *Relative prices of other goods (both related goods and substitutes).* Consumers' demand changes as the price of alternative goods change. For example, with respect to substitutes, imagine how much butter would be sold if suddenly the price of margarine were doubled or tripled. Similarly, to understand the effects of related goods, imagine what effect VHS tape players have had on the movie theater business.
- *Number of consumers.* Consumers' demand is a function of the number of consumers in a market. For example, as the baby boomers matured during the 1970s and 1980s, the number of consumers purchasing new homes rose considerably, with a coinciding increase in housing prices in the 1970s and

1980s. As the baby-boomer generation came of age, there were more buyers for houses which affected the price consumers were willing to pay.

- *Expectations of change.* Consumers react in the market in relation to expectations of future market conditions. For example, when stock investors receive news that could adversely affect the price of their stocks (e.g., changes in prime interest rates), they often react by either buying or selling whether or not the market is ultimately effected. For example, with the onset of Desert Storm, the price of crude oil was expected to skyrocket. Even though there was no real change in oil supplies, the willingness of consumers to shift their buying patterns in response to their expectations had a great market impact.

Similarly, the supply function for any good is governed by the *law of supply,* which states that sellers are willing to provide more of any given good at higher prices than at lower prices given constant supply parameters; these supply parameters and their effects are as follows:

- *Number of producers.* More suppliers mean more goods are available and vice versa. For example, as more suppliers have entered the personal computer market, the price of computers has changed drastically as compared to when there were only a few suppliers.

- *State of technology.* Suppliers will employ any technology which will enable them to produce goods at the lower cost to maximize profits. For example, the price of a very simple, basic hand-held calculator in the 1970s was in the $100 range. However, with increased technology, suppliers can currently provide calculators with those same capabilities at 4 to 6 percent of the previous price.

- *Size of capital stock.* Because suppliers need capital to make improvements and employ new technologies, the availability of capital directly affects the market prices. For example, rising and lowering interest rates (which changes the availability of capital) can drastically affect the ability of suppliers to move into new markets. Thus, interest rates are used by the federal reserve to control supply and, in turn, inflation.

- *Price of inputs.* Suppliers must pass production costs to the consumers via market price. Recall the effect on market prices for any petroleum-based product during and after the oil embargo of the 1970s.

- *Expectations of change.* Suppliers react to perceived changes in markets in the same manner as consumers. This factor forms the basis for futures markets. The price of commodities such as produce can change greatly given the expectation of low harvests due to the possibility of poor weather.

These laws of supply and demand are only empirical; however, they have stood the test of time and are used in market analysis throughout the field of microeconomics. When these functions are combined with the assumption that supply and demand can be represented as a snapshot in time, which implies the supply and demand parameters are constant, both the supply and demand functions can be represented graphically as shown in Fig. 1-1. These functions are specific to both the individual good and the market and can be used to indicate the quantity of the good which will be supplied and demanded at any given price.

In addition, the supply and demand functions can be used to show the equilibrium position for any particular good. By definition, *equilibrium* is established when the quantity of a good supplied is equal to the quantity of a good consumed, i.e., the point of intersection where the functions cross. In referring to the fig-

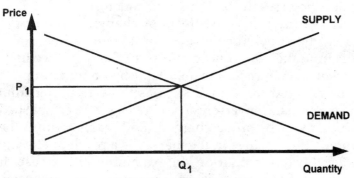

Figure 1-1. Theoretical supply and demand relationship.

ure, it is the point shown where Q_1 is supplied and consumed
(i.e., the market clears) at a price P_1.

Although the exact shapes of the supply and demand functions can vary, those shapes have little effect on this analysis.
Because these functions are shown as a snapshot in time, their
general shapes can be determined by the governing laws of supply and demand. The demand curve must be negatively sloping
to satisfy the requirement that more of a good or service will be
consumed at lower prices. Similarly, the supply curve must
have a positive slope to show that the quantity of a good or service supplied will increase at higher prices.

One of the most startling factors arising from this analysis is
also one that is often overlooked in the business world; these
functions are independent of one another. In other words,
demand cannot create supply, and supply cannot create
demand. For either function to change, the supply or demand
parameters which determine the functions must change or the
market must fail to clear (i.e., if all goods offered are not consumed, there will be a surplus). Unless one of these events
occur, the price relationship defined by the supply and demand
functions will remain constant.

If the independence of these functions were not true, there
would never be a condition of a market "glut" or shortage. If
supply could create demand, the excess supplies of the good in
the market would create demand, and the demand would take
care of the excess supply. However, because these functions are
independent, if there is an excess of supply, the only way that it
can be reduced is to reduce price, i.e., lower than shown as P_1 in
Fig. 1-1, which increases the quantity demanded.

Given this information, the effects of changing one of the
parameters on the supply or demand for a good can be examined. To illustrate this, the concepts of price floors and ceilings
shall be presented. A *price floor* is an established minimum price
which can be charged for a good such as those resulting from
agricultural supports. Conversely, a *price ceiling* is an established
maximum price which can be charged. Both cases require the
analyst to predict the change in the market as a result of altering
the static, equilibrium condition. In examining either case, it
must be assumed that prior to the price control being imposed,

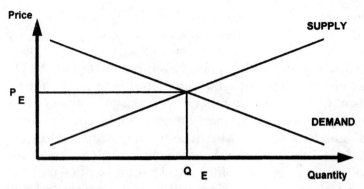

Figure 1-2. Equilibrium market position.

there was an equilibrium situation in the market with the quantity of goods demanded and the quantity supplied being equal as shown in Fig. 1-2.

A price floor is a minimum price that can be charged for a commodity or good. A price floor occurs commonly with respect to price fixing of any type such as a regulatory authority determining that something should not be sold for a price less than a preset minimum. Hence, if a price floor is required, it can be assumed that the minimum price (P) would have had to be above the equilibrium price (P_E) when the action was taken. If the going price (P_E) had been higher than the desired minimum price, there would be no need for the price floor. This implies that the situation shown in Fig. 1-3 would exist.

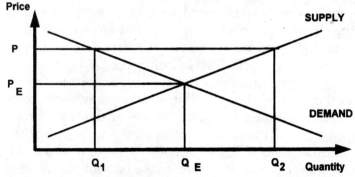

Figure 1-3. The effect of a price floor (minimum price).

Since the imposed price is above the equilibrium price, the quantity demanded by consumers in the market would be reduced from Q_E to Q_1, but, because of this same artificial price, suppliers would increase the quantity supplied from Q_E to Q_2. The overall effect of imposing the price floor is to create a market surplus of $Q_2 - Q_1$, which must be purchased by the government as the agency which imposed the price floor. This purchase of "excess" goods is required because regulation instead of the market was used to set the price which in turn determined the quantity of goods supplied. Since equilibrium implies that the market must clear, to maintain equilibrium at the regulated price, the excess goods must be purchased by the government. Then, once the excess is purchased, they must be either stored, discarded, or given away outside the market. Adding them back into the market would alter the supply function by creating an additional supplier. This problem can clearly be seen in the case of agricultural surpluses due to the farm price supports.

Although in a more complex form, this same situation could easily occur in the environmental arena. If the government were to determine that the amount of high-sulphur coal used as fuel had to be reduced, it could tax each ton of coal purchased. This tax would be an artificial increase in the price of the high-sulphur coal and would have the same effect as a price floor. The consumers of the high-sulphur coal would see a higher price and lower the quantity demanded in the market—the purpose of the legislation. However, the suppliers would continue to produce coal at the lower, no-tax price. The government, to ensure market equilibrium, would be forced to purchase the excess supply. Hence, the tax could have the desired effect of reducing the amount of high-sulphur coal consumed, but, because the market response to the tax was the same as a price floor, other economic impacts must be considered.

Conversely, in some situations those in regulatory authority may perceive the need to place a ceiling or maximum on the price of a good or service. Under the same type of analysis as before, the price ceiling or maximum price would have to be below the market equilibrium price. If this were not true, there would be little reason to set a maximum price above the current equilibrium price. In this case the opposite would result as shown in Fig. 1-4.

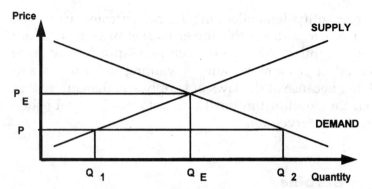

Figure 1-4. The effect of a price ceiling (maximum price).

Because an artificially low maximum price was established in the market, the consumers would increase the quantity demanded to Q_2; however, due to the same artificially low price set by the price ceiling, only Q_1 would be supplied. This situation would cause a market shortage of the commodity equal to $Q_2 - Q_1$. Hence, a number of consumers would demand the good who could not obtain same. This situation could potentially occur in any subsidy situation such as if the government were to provide "free" health care. As shown with just this simple analysis, these situations require that a number of potential drawbacks be addressed. For example, in the case of health care, if the price of health care for consumers suddenly became zero, the quantity of health care demanded would be maximized. However, the quantity supplied would be controlled by the prices paid to the medical providers (i.e., the set prices paid by the government). The only way that the supply could be increased to meet the demand would be to maximize the price paid to the supplier.

To see the effect in an environmental situation, the desire to limit the use of high-sulphur coal can again be used. In the previous example, the regulatory agency opted to place a floor or minimum price on the price of high-sulphur coal. Conversely, the same effect of decreasing demand and use of high-sulphur coal could be accomplished if the regulator set a price ceiling or maximum price on the price of *low*-sulphur coal. In this second scenario, the consumer would see a lower market price and increase the quantity demanded, the desired outcome. However, the supplier would also see this lower market price and reduce the quantity supplied. As before, such regulation would have the desired effect of more consumers wanting to burn low-sulphur coal, but because of the laws of supply and demand within the market, the equilibrium position could not be established without further intervention.

Consumer Surplus

The negatively sloping demand and positively sloping supply functions also lead to the possibility of a selective versus free market. Instead of supplying goods at an equilibrium price, the slopes of these functions imply that if suppliers could single out consumers and sell their goods one at a time, they could increase their profit. If the first unit offered by a supplier were offered to the individual consumer most willing to pay for the good, the maximum price would be paid. In other words, if the consumers could be coupled individually with the suppliers, the first unit of a commodity could be sold at a higher price than the second unit, the second unit at a higher price than the next, and so on, as shown in Fig. 1-5.

Although this would serve to maximize revenue for suppliers, unfortunately, or fortunately for consumers, with the exception

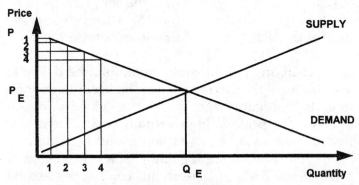

Figure 1-5. Individual pricing of goods.

of a very few luxury goods such as custom-built automobiles, this individual selling is far too cumbersome to be practiced in the market (imagine selling soft drinks one unit at a time). As a result, most goods are offered to the entire market place at the single, equilibrium price. This single equilibrium price does, however, indicate that there is a benefit to the consumer. Since there are consumers who would have been willing to pay more than the equilibrium price for the good, this pricing system is actually beneficial to the consumer.

The area below the demand curve represents the monies that consumers would have been willing to pay for the goods, i.e., price ($/unit) times quantity (units) = total monies paid ($) or the maximum revenue for the suppliers. However, because of the difficulties in individual pricing, the actual monies paid for all the goods consumed is the area below the equilibrium price straight line representing the price. The difference in these amounts, the area below the demand curve and above the equilibrium price, represents either monies consumers would have been willing to spend but did not have to in order to consume the good or service or the actual supplier's revenues versus the maximum revenues. This area has been dubbed consumer surplus (CS).

If consumer surplus is the difference between the total monies consumers are willing to pay for goods and services and the actually monies paid, consumer surplus can be looked upon as being a benefit that results from purchasing in the market place. In an analogous situation, a shopper finding an item on sale could be thought of as a type of consumer surplus. If one would have been willing to pay $50 for a shirt or blouse, and the item was unexpectedly on sale for $35, purchasing the garment would provide $15 worth of consumer surplus (the surplus being the difference between what the consumer was willing to pay and what was actually paid). As done with supply and demand, consumer surplus can be easily shown graphically as done in Fig. 1-6 superimposed over the theoretical supply-demand relationship previously discussed.

Since consumer surplus represents monies consumers did not have to spend, it is considered a benefit to the consumer. Hence, if changes in consumer surplus could be predicted either over

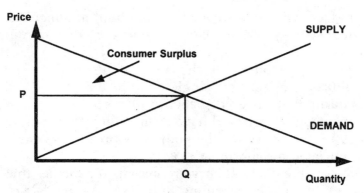

Figure 1-6. Consumer surplus for a good in equilibrium at price *P.*

time or as a result of changing a demand-supply parameter at a given time, these changes could be and have been used as an indicator of consumer welfare. If consumer surplus increases, so does consumer welfare and vice versa. To illustrate this effect, Fig. 1-6 can be used as the baseline condition, and the effects on consumer surplus can be examined as a result of price changes.

First, assume a new technology for producing a good was discovered which eliminated hazardous waste generation during manufacture. This would mean that the supplier's production cost would be lowered (i.e., a change in the supply parameter state of technology would have occurred which would change or shift the supply function), and more of the good could be supplied at a lower cost. This would shift the supply curve to the right (or down) with the demand curve remaining unchanged (i.e., no demand parameters were affected). Intuitively, having more of a good available at a lower cost would seem to benefit consumer welfare and, as shown in Fig. 1-7, consumer surplus would increase.

In this case, because the supply parameter changed, the supply curve would shift as indicated by the arrow, the initial quantity supplied (Q_i) would be increased to Q_f, the equilibrium price would be reestablished from P_i to P_f, and consumer surplus would increase from only area 1, to area $1 + 2 + 3 + 4$.

Similarly, assume that there was a change in supply parameters which caused a production cost increase. For example, if a

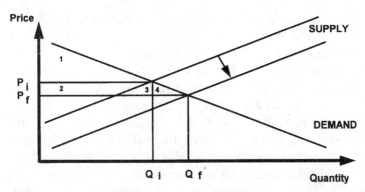

Figure 1-7. Increased consumer surplus as a result of lowered input prices for suppliers.

new environmental requirement were enacted which raised production costs, the supply parameter input cost would change, and the good's supply curve would shift left. As a result of the shift, the quantity demanded and in turn the quantity supplied would decrease, and fewer consumers would choose to purchase the product at the higher price. Again, it is intuitive this would decrease consumer welfare, and, as shown in Fig. 1-8, this is reflected by a reduction in consumer surplus.

In this second case, the change in supply parameters would cause a shift in the supply curve left as indicated by the arrow,

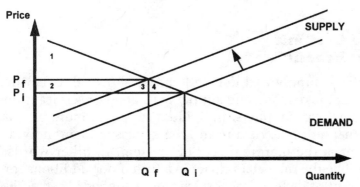

Figure 1-8. Decreased consumer surplus as a result of increased input prices for suppliers.

the initial quantity supplied (Q_i) would be decreased to Q_f, the price would increase from P_i to P_f, and consumer surplus would decrease from areas $1 + 2 + 3 + 4$ to only area 1.

From the above analysis, it is apparent that changes in consumer surplus can be used as a measure to indicate changes in consumer welfare. There are other far more complex techniques for measuring these changes (e.g., compensating variation and equivalent variation), but they are mathematically complex and do little to decrease uncertainty in the analysis. As stated by Freeman (1982a), in most cases the differences in the measures of consumer welfare, consumer surplus, compensating variation, and equivalent variation appear to be small and almost trivial. As a result Freeman (1982a, p. 48) has gone so far as to say, "There is a strong argument for using the ordinary consumer surplus as an empirical approximation [to changes in consumer welfare]."

Therefore, if the change in consumer surplus due to initiating various pollution prevention options could be estimated, the effect could be predicted. However, as shown, such an analysis is based on the supply and demand functions. In that these functions are an aggregate of all consumer's demands and all supplier's efforts within the entire market, they cannot be controlled by any single supplier. To be more useful, these functions must be reduced to the level of individual suppliers and consumers where not only can changes be made but effects on individual suppliers can be predicted.

Marginal Cost and Marginal Benefit

Given that the supply and demand curves shown thus far are aggregates of the demand and supply for a good or service from all consumers and suppliers, individual suppliers more or less face a set market price. As a result, the key issue to an individual supplier is the marginal cost of an item. In other words, what would be the financial impact to a firm if one additional or one fewer unit of the good or service were supplied? If an additional unit can be supplied at a cost less than the benefit derived from its sale (i.e., if the marginal cost is less than the equilibrium market price), the supplier should increase production. Conversely, if an additional unit would cost the supplier more than can be recovered from the unit's sale, the good should not be produced. This concept involves unit pricing and, depending on whether the cost or the benefit of producing the single additional unit is the subject of inquiry, it is referred to as the *marginal cost* or *marginal benefit*.

Although this seems like a simple concept, it is often difficult to establish "benefits" in working through an analysis. In the case of a market equilibrium price, the marginal benefit of producing an additional unit is easy to predict in that it is simply the market price of the good. However, the environmental arena provides a number of more complex issues, and there is no "equilibrium price." For example, assume a town had an inadequate sanitary wastewater treatment plant which resulted in pollutant emissions to the local river. To compute the marginal benefit and cost, first, the current amount of pollution emitted to the river must be established. Then, the cost to the environment (i.e., damage to the river) from each unit of pollution emitted would be estimated. Although actually assigning a dollar value to costs such as "environmental damage to the river" can be very difficult, it is possible through any number of microeconomic techniques. Thus, the cost of environmental damage, the cost side of a marginal benefit–marginal cost analysis, would be established.

To determine whether or to what degree the water treatment plant should be modernized or upgraded, the opposing variable's curve, the cost of controlling each additional unit of pollution, must be established. Fortunately, this is a relatively simple design problem with specific costs being assigned to secondary or tertiary treatment methods; information that is readily available from engineers and manufactures. Then all that is required is to compare the cost of improved water quality with the additional treatment to the cost of environmental damage.

It may appear that this represents a cost-cost versus cost-benefit analysis because there is a cost associated with additional water treatment (construction, maintenance, operations, etc.) and a cost associated with environmental damage. However, it actually is a cost-benefit balancing act. In this type of situation, the environmental "cost" from discharging polluted water is most often treated as a benefit by expressing the "cost" as damage not sustained due to the effluent discharge. Hence, in the above example, the benefit of avoiding environmental damage by the additional treatment is balanced against the additional cost of modernizing the treatment plant.

Such marginal cost-benefit analyses have a number of uses to determine the optimal operating level for any financial situation. As an illustration, suppose a city wanted to optimize the level of law enforcement it employed. For simplicity, assume that the unit for law enforcement can be represented by a "cop" so the graphical representation for the analysis will be a continuous function.

First, the two extremes or endpoints of the marginal cost and marginal benefit curves must be established. To first establish the marginal cost curve for law enforcement, consider the case where there are zero cops. If there were no law enforcement, the cost of law enforcement would be zero. Conversely, cops could be added one unit at a time (at least theoretically), to the point where there was 100 percent law enforcement (i.e., zero crime). However, at this zero crime point, the cost of cops would be maximized. Hence, the end points for the marginal cost curve are established; zero cost at 0 percent crime control and some very high value at 100 percent crime control.

Similarly, to establish the marginal benefit curve, the cost of crime, viewed as the benefit of not having crime, could be established. If there were no cops, the cost of crime would be maximized. Conversely, if there were 100 percent crime control, the cost of crime would be zero. Hence, the endpoints for both functions have been established. This relationship is shown in Fig. 1-9.

Once this relationship is established, a government can set the cost—the level of crime control—or the benefit—the cost due to crime to be avoided—at any point it wishes by simply adding or subtracting cops until it reaches the optimal situation. To optimize the government's investment in crime control, it should continue to increase the number of cops as long as the marginal benefit derived from the expenditure (i.e., the benefit of controlling one additional unit of crime) was greater than the cost of

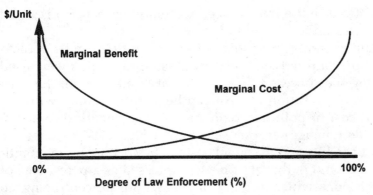

Figure 1-9. The marginal cost–marginal benefit for law enforcement.

providing that same additional unit of enforcement. Although this seems like a simple concept, it has far reaching consequences as shall be examined in the following environmental example.

This relationship between marginal cost and benefit and supply and demand in an environmental analysis is equally straightforward; cost relates to supply, and benefit relates to demand. If the supply and demand curves represent the total, aggregate supply and demand for a good, to find the marginal cost–marginal benefit, one merely has to examine the change in the values over a single additional unit (i.e., take the derivative of the supply or demand curve). Mathematically, this can be complex; however, on an empirical basis, this is a logical conclusion. It is easy to conceptualize that consumers would not purchase a good if the benefit derived from consuming the good was less than the cost (i.e., the marginal cost was greater than the marginal benefit).

Defining Social Optimum

In an economic sense, social optimum can be defined as the market condition where the marginal cost associated with a good or service is equal to the marginal benefit derived from same. For example, basic economic theory predicts that a consumer will purchase any given good until the marginal utility received from that purchase (i.e., the marginal benefit) is equal to the price paid for the unit of the good.

In a similar sense, the same optimal condition can be applied to pollution control. Using the same assumptions that were used in shaping the curves in the example of crime control, the marginal cost of pollution control can be graphed along with the marginal cost of pollution damage (i.e., the benefit of not sustaining the damage) on one set of axes. Figure 1-10 shows the marginal benefits and marginal costs as a function of the quantity of pollution (Q), the latter being expressed as a percentage of total emissions which are controlled, with 0 percent being no control (marginal cost equal to zero) and 100 percent being no emissions (marginal cost maximized).

In Fig. 1-10, the optimum point, the point where the two curves intersect, is of critical importance and is designated by the quantity of pollution emitted, Q^*. At this point, the marginal costs to control emissions are equal to the marginal benefit of avoiding the damage which would have been caused had the pollutant been emitted. Any control efforts in excess of those needed to obtain Q^* (i.e., pollution quantities to the right of Q^* as shown in Fig. 1-10), would result in the marginal cost of control being higher than the marginal benefit of avoiding the damage which would have been sustained. In other words, the cost would outweigh the benefit received. Similarly, if more

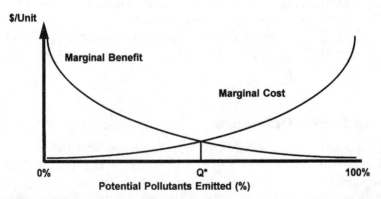

Figure 1-10. Marginal control–marginal benefit for controlling pollutant emissions.

than Q^* pollution were allowed (i.e., pollution control exercised to the left of Q^* in the Fig.), the damage to the environment would be greater than the cost of control. Hence, in a social context, only at Q^* does the benefit of pollution control equal the cost, which is, by definition, the optimum level of pollution control.

Establishing the social optimum at the point of marginal cost equal to marginal benefit seems logical; however, it carries the significant implication that 100 percent pollution control, i.e., zero emissions, is not a desirable end. This is because, again in a social context, more resources would be would have to be dedicated to the process of controlling pollution than the benefits derived from having less pollution could support. Hence, from the individual supplier's perspective, the optimal monies spent on any pollution control measure (i.e., the combined costs of control efforts, monitoring, environmental damage, and so on) should be set where the marginal cost of pollution control is equal to the marginal benefit as shown in Fig. 1-10.

Establishing the marginal cost curve for emission control is a relatively easy task in that the prices for control equipment, labor, maintenance, are available from vendors and design engineers for any level of pollution control. Conversely, computing the benefit curve representing the benefits derived from avoiding damage can be quite complex. In determining the "worth" of cleaner air or cleaner water, aesthetics, wildlife, and the like in addition to health issues must be included in the analysis. Fortunately, that is normally the job of the regulatory community, and the individual environmental manager does not need to consider the problem. The only matter of importance to the supplier is the point of intersection of the two curves, and the regulators will indicate this by taxes, emission limits, and so on, so the analysis from the suppliers' viewpoint will be much like having an equilibrium price instead of a marginal benefit curve.

As a case study to show how the marginal benefit curves are expressed to suppliers, how various options can be examined, and how regulators and suppliers must view different strategies, a scenario examining control options for air pollution from a stationary source shall be examined.

Case Study: Optimizing Air Pollution Control

The government has taken on the responsibility of providing the nation with clean, breathable air. However, there are a number of methods which regulatory agencies can use to impose the required amount of pollution control on suppliers.

Instruments to Achieve Air Pollution Control

Command and Control (CAC).   In the scheme of pollution regulation, there are the polluters, who are responsible for reducing pollution, and the regulators, who are responsible for allocating the control responsibility among the pollution sources and enforcing the pollution requirements. Traditionally, this has been done by establishing a separate emission standard for each source which discharges a given pollutant. This method of regulation has been dubbed *command and control* (CAC). Conceptually, this method relies on setting an emission control requirement on each source which, if met and maintained, would result in the desired air quality.

Although this may seem like a straightforward method to control emissions and maintain air quality, there were 27,000+ major stationary air pollution sources in the United States in 1994, which makes the task of allocating emission standards formidable at the very least. In addition to the problems associated with the shear number of sources, the government must seek the optimal economic control point to maximize the benefit to society. In other words, the total monies spent on pollution control must be equal to the total benefit derived from the damage the environment does not sustain. Assuming the regulator can establish a single marginal benefit curve for air pollution, achieving the optimum solution requires that the marginal cost of emission control be set at the same point for all pollutant sources (at the point where marginal cost is equal to marginal benefit). Given the diversity of the sources for any given air pollutant and the variety of marginal costs within similar firms or industries, optimizing emission control under this option requires the regulator to have knowledge of all marginal costs for all emitters of the pollutant, an information load that is nearly impossible to obtain and manage.

This information requirement points to one of the major problems in a CAC situation. The marginal cost information needed by the regulators to optimize emission control is known only by the polluters. As a result, when reporting cost data, the polluters have a strong incentive to overstate or pad the actual costs of control in hopes of acquiring a relaxed emission requirement for their firm. Hence, the fundamental problem with the CAC method is an information mismatch between responsibilities for the two major players.

The emission limit approach under CAC imposes the responsibility on the regulator to assign specific emission limits to each source so that the air quality standards would be maintained if the emission limits were met. However, given that full marginal control cost data must be know to set emission levels, it would be extremely difficult to establish individual emission limits which would provide optimal environmental control from an economic standpoint. Conversely, a single standard for a given pollutant could be establish across an industry. For example, Fig. 1-11 shows two hypothetical firms with the same emission limit which are engaged in the same industry but have different marginal control costs for a given pollutant.

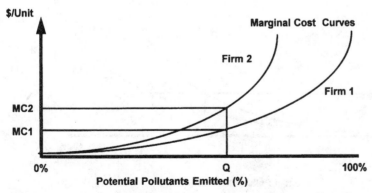

Figure 1-11. The effect of constant emission limits on firms with different marginal control costs.

If the regulatory agency were to set specific, identical emission limits in terms of pollutant discharge on the two firms, for example Q in Fig. 1-11, firm 1 would obviously be in a much better financial position than firm 2 because firm 1's marginal control costs are lower. In this case, firm 2 would oppose regulation based on the concept that the regulators are adversely affecting its market position by raising its costs more than their competitors.

Conversely, the regulator could establish different standards for the two firms so that they both would operate at the same marginal cost. This situation is shown in Fig. 1-12.

In this latter case, both firms are forced to operate at the economic optimal level in that their marginal costs for control are both equal to MC. However, in this case, firm 1 (as represented by MC1) would control at the point Q_1 and firm 2 (as represented by MC2) would be forced to control more emissions at the point Q_2. Hence, firm 1 would oppose the regulator by making the case that it was being discriminated against in that it had to control more emissions than its competitor. It is apparent through this analysis that the level of emissions, if set by the regulator through directive, automatically establishes a valid basis for complaint.

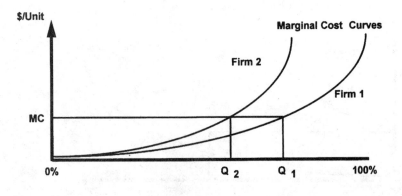

Figure 1-12. The effect of equalizing marginal costs on firms with different marginal control cost curves.

Emissions Fees. An alternative to setting specific emission limits, as is done under CAC, would be to set a fee per unit of pollution emitted by an individual pollutant source. Simply put, emissions by polluters would not be controlled in that they could emit any amount of pollution they desired as long as they were willing to pay the fee for each unit of emission. This may seem like a poor solution; however, in a free market economy, suppliers which seek to maximize profit will also attempt to achieve the same optimum point of marginal cost equal to marginal benefit. This implies that rather than operating without constraining pollutant emissions, a supplier would control emissions up to the point where the marginal cost of emission control equalled the marginal benefit of control (i.e., to the point where the marginal control cost was equal to the price of the fee). As a result, in maximizing profit, suppliers would automatically move to the point where they would emit pollutants up to the point Q^* in Fig. 1-10. There would be no incentive for firms to control emissions beyond that point because the marginal cost of controlling an additional unit of pollutant would be higher than the fee the firms would pay for emitting the pollutant. Similarly, firms would not emit pollutants greater than Q^* (i.e., control fewer emissions) because the cost of paying the emission fee would be greater than the marginal cost of controlling the pollutant. As a result, each supplier would automatically set their level of pollution control to the point where MC = fee, the economic optimum.

The problem in administering this method of regulatory control becomes apparent when the regulators attempt to establish the marginal cost–marginal benefit functions (the curves shown in Fig. 1-10) so they can determine the level at which to set the fee. The marginal benefit function representing the environmental damage avoided by pollutants not emitted is set by the government and, as stated before, can be established unilaterally by the regulator with the resources available. Conversely, establishing the marginal cost of control curve again requires the regulator to have complete knowledge of the marginal control costs for all sources; the same information mismatch that was apparent in the case of CAC.

In addition, even if the regulator could establish all of the polluter's marginal costs, there is a problem with applying the emission limit. Under both systems, CAC and fees, regulators are forced to control pollutant emissions in that emission rates are the most easily measured quantity. Hence, the regulator simply sets a single fee for all polluters. This simplicity of a single fee is the real advantage under this regulatory option in that it negates the requirement for knowing each polluter's emission costs. However, the amount of the fee that is set will also control the amount of emissions. Hence, the key issue is whether the emissions resulting from each polluter optimizing their control will result in the desired air quality. Again, given the large number of sources, each with an individual marginal cost curve, this becomes a difficult undertaking given the amount of information required. Further, the same basis for polluter's complaints as explored under the CAC option (shown in Figs. 1-11 and 1-12) would occur if the regulatory agency were to establish either unequal fees among similar sources or a single fee with unequal emission standards. As a result, the problems of information overload, mismatch of information between capabilities and responsibilities of the players, and the inherent basis for complaint is much the same with fees as it was for CAC.

Marketable Permits.   The final control option currently available to the regulatory community is that of marketable permits. In essence, the permit is a license to pollute which allows the holder to emit any amount of pollutant up to the level specified in the marketable permit. If only the permissible amount of pollution is emitted, the air quality will be maintained.

This implies that the regulatory goal of obtaining the air quality goals under the marketable permit scenario is greatly simplified. All that the regulator needs to establish is the total amount of pollution that can be discharged into a given air shed based on the ambient air quality desired in a given area or region. Then, marketable permits which allow that pollution loading would be made available to the polluters. The polluters would then obtain any number of permits they desire through the market system.

From the economically optimal viewpoint, because polluters are attempting to maximize profit, their demand for permits (and, in turn the level of pollution control exercised by each polluter) would automatically move to the socially optimal level. Polluters would simply purchase permits, at a fair market price, until the cost of the permit was equal to their individual marginal costs for environmental control. Although this means that some firms could be polluting more than others, there is no basis for an individual supplier to complain given that any firm is free to obtain more permits on the open market.

From the regulatory standpoint, the method to deal with enforcement is also simplified. Given that the premise used to establish the number of permits available in any region was based on the capability of the region to assimilate the pollution, the overall ambient air quality standard will be automatically maintained (assuming the polluters remained within their permitted emissions). Further, the system would automatically operate at the socially optimal level, because all polluters seeking to maximize profit would operate at the point where their marginal costs and benefits were equal (marginal control costs equal to the market price of the permit).

The most striking aspect of this method of emission control is that the regulator does not need information regarding the individual polluter's marginal control costs. The only information required is an ambient air quality standard to be achieved. Then, based on meteorologic data, fate and transport modeling, and so on, the maximum emission load can be computed. Hence, this method avoids the information mismatch between the polluter's and regulator's responsibilities and capabilities that occurred under CAC.

There are however limitations under a permit system. The marketable permit case, as is the case with most microeconomic analyses, assumes that a perfectly competitive market existed in which trades between polluters for additional permits could take place freely and that no individual supplier could control the market (no monopoly would exist). In that these assumptions are never 100 percent correct, the actual benefits of marketable permits could be overstated in any theoretical analysis; however, it is useful to continue this comparison of the three potential regulatory approaches, CAC, fees, and permits, to see how economics can be used to compare how the implementation of each strategy could affect the following areas:

- Can the regulatory approach achieve the socially and economically optimum level of air emissions control?
- Can the regulatory approach serve as an incentive to the development of new pollution control technologies?
- Are the costs associated with each regulatory option (e.g., information gathering, monitoring, and enforcement) prohibitive?

For simplicity, the analysis shall continue to be limited to air pollution control. However, the same arguments and discussions used herein apply equally well to water pollution, land pollution, and so on, with only minor changes.

Achieving Social Optimum Control

Command and Control. As indicated previously, the information burden inherent to command and control in achieving the socially optimum control where all firms have equal marginal costs is overwhelming. In addition, if after setting an emission standard for a firm, the ambient air quality is not achieved, the regulator has little recourse against the polluters—they are each emitting pollution at their legal level.

Emissions Fees. In this case, each firm will automatically control emissions to the level where its individual marginal costs are equal to the price of the fee so social optimality is achieved. However, this method also requires a great deal of information on the part of regulators to enable them to establish the fee at the proper level to attain and maintain the ambient air quality standard. Hence, although optimal from the polluter's standpoint (i.e., fee = MC), the resulting air quality may not be satisfactory.

Marketable Permits. In issuing permits, the regulator determines how much pollution, from all sources, can be assimilated by the environment and still maintain the ambient air quality standards. Then permits which allow that much pollution are issued. In this manner, the regulator is guaranteed that the air quality standard will be met (assuming the mixing, transport, and similar calculations were accurate), and the regulator does not need to be concerned with who gets the permit. In the market system, firms with high marginal control costs will seek to purchase additional permits. Firms who can receive prices for the permits they own, in excess of their marginal control costs, will sell same. Hence, at equilibrium, each firm will be operating its pollution control equipment at the level where the market permit price is equal to the firm's individual marginal control costs. Since each permit holder is free to buy or sell permits, all firms would be operating at the point of equal marginal costs; social optimality and air quality would be achieved.

Incentives for Technology Development

Command and Control. In this case, all polluters are operating at the emission level to which they are legally bound. Assuming that additional pollution control cannot be achieved without cost, there is no profit incentive for any behavior other than business as usual. With no incentive to reduce emission rates beyond the current control levels, CAC holds no incentive for the development of improved control technologies.

Fees. To understand the profit incentive for technological development, the effect of a changing marginal cost curve on the amount of fee paid, and in turn on the control costs for the firm, must be examined. Figure 1-13 shows a firm with an initial mar-

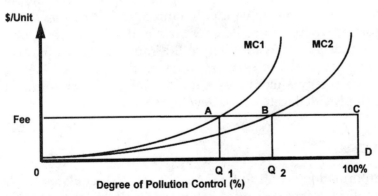

Figure 1-13. The effects of adding a new, more efficient pollution control technology.

ginal control cost curve of MC1 and a potential cost curve, if new emission control equipment were installed, of MC2.

If a firm was initially operating on MC1, under a regulatory system of fees, it would naturally move to the point where it emits Q_1 pollutants. Therefore, the total control costs paid by the firm could be represented by the area bounded by 0-A-Q_1 and total amount of fees paid by the area bounded by A-C-D-Q_1. If a new technology became available which would lower the control costs (i.e., shift the marginal control cost curve right to MC2), the firm would have a completely different situation. If the new equipment were installed, the firm would be paying control costs equivalent to the area 0-B-Q_2 and fees equivalent to the area B-C-D-Q_2; a savings equivalent to the area 0-A-B. Hence, with the incentive to lower the total costs, the firm would have the incentive to apply new control technologies. The result would be either increased profit or an improved competitive position for the firm's goods or services. This would result in a demand for new technologies (suppliers would attempt to lower the supply parameter input costs) which would provide the incentive to develop same.

Permits.   As shown above, if there is financial advantage to a supplier to reduce pollution emissions, there will be a market for additional control, and development of new technologies will be stimulated. In the case of marketable permits, the financial advantage is even easier to see. New technology which would lower emissions would mean one of two things to a supplier. The supplier either could continue to emit pollutants at the current level at a lower cost or could reduce its emissions and sell its excess permits. In either case, the supplier could improve its competitive position for its goods or services in its product market. Hence, again this strategy encourages a market for new technologies, which will provide incentive for development.

Control Costs

CAC.   Information is critical for CAC because the regulator needs to have full marginal cost information available to set the allowable emission level for each firm. Hence, the cost of obtaining information is very high, and, to further complicate matters, there is incentive to the polluters to overstate their costs (in hopes of receiving relaxed emission limits).

Similarly, since the sources are regulated versus the ambient air, monitoring each source becomes a major financial undertaking. Even if this monitoring requirement is passed onto the polluter instead of being done by the regulator, this cost must be passed on to the consumer either through higher prices or taxes. In addition, firms could cheat in their monitoring programs. It is true that each firm would limit its emissions to a point where the marginal benefit was equal to the marginal cost; however, the individual polluter does not necessarily see the same marginal benefit. The regulator established the marginal benefit as the benefit to society of pollution damage avoided. Instead, supplier's individual financial analysis of marginal benefit could relate to the cost of not getting caught in a noncompliance situation. If there is little monitoring effort on the part of the regulator, this price of getting caught (a probability function), can take on a very low value which implies little pollution control (i.e., low benefit = low MC). Hence, monitoring can be a major expense.

Conversely, the transaction costs for this alternative are very attractive. Given that the only transaction required is to assign emission limits to the sources, they are very low.

Fees. As in the case of CAC, information is critical if the fees are to be set to the point where each firm operating at an optimal level (i.e., fee = MC) will result in the desired ambient air quality. Although economically optimum conditions are guaranteed, a specific overall emission load is related to each fee level. Hence, the marginal control cost information for each supplier is still required by the regulator to set the fee and in turn achieve the desired ambient air quality.

As in the case of CAC, without regulatory monitoring, there will be incentives to cheat by understating the emissions to reduce the fees that a firm must pay. However, unlike CAC, the regulatory agencies could easily establish general guidelines which could be monitored based on the amount of fee paid given the control equipment installed. For example, if the areal average fee for coal-fired power plants with electrostatic precipitators was X, and one plant paid less, it could be easily flagged for investigation at the time the fees are recorded. Hence, monitoring could not be eliminated; however, the system has a built in check-and-balance mechanism.

Transaction costs would be higher than those under the CAC option. Once the fee systems were established, not only would the fees have to be assessed (an equivalent transaction cost to the CAC option), but they would have to be collected, accounted for, and so on.

Permits. In this simplified analysis, a permit system combines the best of all worlds. With respect to information requirements, the regulators need only two pieces of information, which are within their control—the ambient air quality standards to be met and general modeling information regarding the total pollutant load that can be assimilated by the environment. The requirement for individual polluter's marginal cost information is eliminated under this option.

Monitoring under a system of permits is inherently easier than with other options. Because the emphasis of the permit option is on concentration (i.e., ambient air quality) versus emissions, the regulator need only monitor specific points within the air shed. As long as the air quality is at an acceptable level, there is no need for further monitoring. In addition, there is less incentive for firms to control at levels less than allowed under the permits because at an equilibrium market condition there are no buyers for permits at the market price and hence limited financial incentive for selling permits. Conversely, if ambient air quality standards were not met, finding the guilty polluter would require the same monitoring as needed using a command and control strategy.

Transaction costs would be considerably higher under this final option because as permit trades and sales were made between polluters, they would have to be tracked, recorded, and so on; however, these costs would automatically be assimilated in the market price and would not be a burden on the regulator. This is because the firm would naturally include transaction costs in the expense involved in obtaining the permit, and the socially optimal level of marginal cost equal to marginal benefit would be obtained. From the regulator's standpoint, there is no need for involvement in the actual exchange of permits save a verification of the analyses done by the exchange participants to ensure their exchange would maintain the ambient air quality standard.

Summary

This brief analysis indicates the importance and benefit of a firm establishing and operating at the social optimum point of marginal costs equal to marginal benefits. In this specific case, the analysis indicates that a system of marketable permits could be very advantageous. However, these benefits are constrained by a number of variables that were not taken into account in the analysis such as the assumption of a free market, spacial impacts of trades outside of individual air sheds, and temporal issues. However, this analysis indicates that there could be a potential benefit in moving to a system of marketable permits. Even if the result were only a modest savings in the range of a few percent, the overall effect could be substantial given the predicted $50 billion compliance cost for the new Clean Air Act.

The critical aspect is that with just the simple tools introduced in the section, marginal cost, marginal benefit, optimality, and so on, a number of insights into the financial advantages and disadvantages of potential business decisions appear. For example, the graph developed in Fig. 1-12 would clearly indicate the potential savings of using a new technology. This savings could then be compared to the initial cost of implementation to make a business decision.

Externalities

In microeconomic analysis, an externality exists in the market place whenever one consumer's actions involuntarily depend on the actions of another. This dependence can result in either a benefit or a cost, but it must be a result beyond the control of one of the affected consumers in the market. Pollution of the environment is the classic example of a negative externality. For example, a negative externality would exist if the effluent generated during the production process were freely released to a public body of water. The consumers, society, would have an involuntary cost due to the pollution; however, unless the polluter were held financially accountable, this additional cost would not enter into the polluter's financial decision process. Without accountability for the environmental damage born by the consumers, the producer would not include the cost of pollution in determining the optimal point for production. Since the cost of pollution would not be included in the producer's marginal cost calculation, a negative externality would exist.

Similarly, positive externalities can occur, but they seldom arise in the environmental arena. For example, IBM has an excellent training program for its employees. If another producer were to hire an IBM employee, it could take advantage of the benefit of the employee's training, but the marginal cost of that training would not be a factor for the hiring company. Hence, it has enjoyed a benefit that was involuntarily caused by another party in the market place, a benefit of training which did not enter into its economic decision. As in the case of negative externalities, normal market pricing is unable to provide just compensation because the prices do not account for all the costs associated with the transaction.

**Externalities and
Consumer Surplus**

In a pollution scenario, the concept of negative externalities can be combined with consumer surplus to show the effects on social welfare. Recalling the supply function shown in Fig. 1-2, a good in equilibrium in the market, the effects of an externality can be superimposed over the market equilibrium graph. Assuming that in supplying a good to the market place the producer polluted the air or water and did not have to pay that cost, a negative externality would exist. Hence, although the producer would only view the costs represented by the supply function in Fig. 1-2, from a social context, the actual cost of producing the good not only would be the cost that the producer considers but also must include the external or societal costs. Figure 1-14 shows this total cost (TC), equal to the producer cost (C_p) plus the cost of the externality (C_e), superimposed on the equilibrium position.

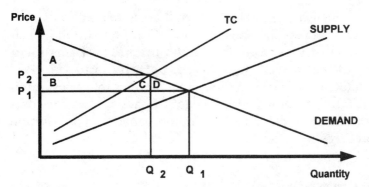

Figure 1-14. Change in consumer surplus due to negative externalities.

The overall effect is identical to the case shown earlier when the supply curve was shifted left due to increased producer costs. The addition of an externality decreases the level of consumer surplus from areas $A + B + C + D$ to only area A. In addition, the quantity supplied by the producer (Q_1) would be too great given the unaccounted social cost and should be decreased to Q_2 with an associated price increase from P_1 to P_2 to reflect the total societal cost. Negative externalities cause overproduction, under-pricing, and reduced consumer surplus because the market system, as seen by the producer, does not include social costs.

The general approach to remedy the negative externality situation is to impose legislation which forces the polluter to internalize the social cost of production into the firm, thereby forcing firms to consider total cost in their marginal cost analysis. This can be done directly, which was shown in the case of levying a fee for each unit of pollutant emitted discussed earlier, or indirectly. In an indirect approach, regulations can be levied which limit pollutant discharges to the air and water under a command and control scenario. This is currently practiced through regulations such as the Clean Air Act and Clean Water Act, which limit the amount of pollutants which can be discharged. This limitation forces polluters to treat their waste effluents to preset standards. Therefore, they are forced to consider treatment costs, as a proxy for environmental damage costs, as part of their marginal cost analyses.

This concept of internalizing external costs through environmental regulation sets the stage for pollution prevention investment. Because of these regulatory requirements, firms incur costs for pollution treatment, fees, permits, and the like. Suppliers look at these costs in the same manner they view environmental damage not sustained as a benefit. Control costs which are not incurred can be considered benefits in a pollution prevention investment analysis.

Public vs. Private Goods

The existence of externalities, and in turn the ability of the market to reflect the total cost without additional regulation, is determined by whether the goods can be categorized as public or private. This categorization centers around two concepts: *indivisibility* and *excludability*.

A good is indivisible when a unit of the good can be consumed by one individual without detracting, in the slightest, from the consumption opportunities still available to others. An example of a perfectly indivisible good would be a panoramic view. Any number of people can enjoy a beautiful sunset, yet the view is still available for all other consumers. Conversely, if consumption of a good fully eliminates consumption on the part of other consumers (such as with foodstuffs), it is considered perfectly divisible.

Excludability of a good depends upon the control a supplier can exercise over consumption or over the number of consumers which can derive the benefits from the good. If the benefits of a good can be costlessly withheld by the supplier from any consumer who does not pay, the good is said to be excludable. This excludability forms the basis of the market system in that in order to set and obtain a price for a good, there must be a means of excluding those who do not pay the price. Again, foodstuffs are the classic example of an excludable good.

Based on these concepts, private goods are defined as goods whose benefits are divisible and excludable (i.e., goods which are singularly consumable and benefits can be withheld), whereas public goods are those whose benefits are indivisible and unexcludable. For example, a supermarket handles private goods in that only those who pay for the goods can use them, and once consumed, the goods cannot be used by other consumers. Conversely, the pleasant aroma in the air after a spring rain can be considered a public good in that any and all consumers can enjoy the good without cost (the good cannot be withheld) and without affecting the ability of other consumers to enjoy the fresh air.

Hence, externalities can only exist in situations where public goods are concerned. Legislation and regulation must be keyed to situations where there is a negative effect on public goods such as air sheds, aquifers, and surface waters. Admittedly, there are situations where goods cannot be clearly defined into either category. For example, if excludability is the only problem, a public good can be made private if the benefits derived from consumption are more valuable than the cost of excluding consumers from free use. This is the situation found in private golf courses, private tennis clubs, and the like. In these cases, one consumer's use of the good does not affect the next person's consumption (any number of people can play tennis on a court with negligible damage), so the goods are indivisible; however, they can be made excludable through memberships, green fees, and so on. The key often lies in the ability of the market consumers to define their "ownership" of the good.

Property Rights

Property rights are a natural result of the concept of divisibility and a critical consideration in determining whether an externality exists and whether or not legislation is required. From the basic definitions of externalities, a consumer must incur costs (or benefits) that are not accounted for in the market. In general, this can only occur where there is no definite ownership of the affected commodity or, in the case of environmental damage, there are so many "owners" that a market is impossible to establish.

The ability to fully define property rights hence becomes an important consideration in many externality situations. For example, if a single person lights a fire in a fireplace, the aroma of the smoke may seem to some consumers to be a benefit. However, if a number of persons all light their fireplaces, the air quality may be affected, transforming the benefit into a societal cost. If the consumers of air who were bothered by the smoke held the property rights to the air that was being used as the smoke "dump," these consumers could charge those who use their fireplaces a fee in order to be compensated for the discomfort caused by the smoke pollution. Conversely, if the fireplace owners "owned" the air, those persons affected by the smoke could pay the fireplace users to not use their fireplaces. This latter case would represent a compensation to the users for not being able to enjoy all the fires they otherwise would desire. In either case, the fact that property rights could be established for the commodity or good determined whether a market could exist which internalized all costs.

Hence, when property rights can be and are well defined, the normal free market system can deal with what would otherwise be considered an externality. It is only when consumers do not need to take other's welfare into account in their decisions (i.e. no property rights) that an externality can exist and legislation/regulation is required.

Establishing Marginal Benefit–Marginal Cost Curves

From the definition of optimality that was developed, the marginal cost and marginal benefit curves must be established. In cases where an externality exists, as demonstrated before, the marginal costs for emission control are normally relatively easy to determine from vendors, design engineers, and so on. However, establishing the marginal benefit curve is by no means an easy task. This is because in the case of public goods (such as clean air), there is no naturally occurring market. Hence, to determine the marginal benefit (costs not incurred), a market must be simulated to assign marginal costs.

Simulating a market leads to a number of potential problems depending upon people's intentions. Some of the techniques used to approximate the market are the bidding game, travel cost method, and hedonic pricing. However, it is critical to realize that each method has an inherent shortfall. Since all the methods rely on estimates of worth by consumers rather than actual expenditures, all the methods can lead to distortions and inaccuracies. For example, consumers with strong beliefs regarding a subject may think it necessary to overstate the worth and their willingness to pay. Similarly, some consumers may understate their willingness to pay in an attempt to hold costs down. For example, in estimating the value of clean air if an environmental activist were interviewed one may get an exaggerated estimate of worth based on the individual's strong feelings for the subject. Conversely, if an industrial polluter were interviewed, the response may actually be artificially low in an attempt to lower pollution emission requirements.

Summary

Given the above discussions, it is apparent that if regulatory intervention is required for pollution control, an externality must first be shown to exist. If this is not the case, the market has the ability to make the necessary corrections and ameliorate the situation. Hence, the first step in addressing environmental problems and/or determining whether additional regulation is needed is problem assessment: what type of good is involved (public, private, or something in between); are property rights assigned, or could they be; and is it a situation whereby market arbitration/negotiation can occur. These actions will lead to the identification of an externality which cannot be addressed within the marketplace, and, as a result, this is the first step in addressing environmental problems. Microeconomic analysis can aid in determining both whether legislation is needed and to what level the legislation should be applied.

Once a problem which cannot correct itself via the market has been identified, societal control can be exercised over the polluter to bring about elimination or amelioration of the pollution. The preferred instrument is to internalize the cost to the polluter; however, determining the optimal cost which the polluter must pay is difficult due to the complexity of estimating the marginal benefit curves. Although difficult, the above methods can be readily applied in the case of environmental protection. By internalizing the societal costs, the polluter is forced to include them in financial and economic decision making. In actuality, these actions redefine the marginal cost curves and force the polluters to seek a new point for their marginal cost–marginal benefit optimization.

In determining whether a firm should invest in pollution prevention, the first step is to establish the marginal cost of pollution control and compare that to the benefit of not emitting the pollution. In this analysis, the effects of externalities, social optimization, and the like, all must be considered as well as the potential effects of developing technologies and pending legislation. An understanding of the concepts introduced in this section provides important insight into determining what costs and benefits should be included in an investment analysis.

Study Concepts

1. Be able to determine the shape of the supply-demand curves from the laws of supply and demand.
2. Given a market situation, be able to predict if there is a change in the parameters of supply and/or demand and what the effect will be on the supply and demand functions for the good.
3. Given a supply-demand curve, be able to give the market effects of price floors and of price ceilings.
4. Be able to define consumer surplus and give the rationale for how it is derived.
5. Be able to explain how consumer surplus can be used as an indicator of social welfare and be able to show and explain changes in consumer surplus given changes in the supply and demand functions.
6. Be able to both define the concepts of marginal benefit and marginal costs and identify costs and benefits in an environmental situation.
7. Be able to explain the shape of the marginal cost–marginal benefit curves.
8. Be able to defend the concept that a business operating at the point where marginal cost is equal to marginal benefit is operating at the "optimal" point.
9. Be able to define the microeconomic pros and cons of the three air pollution control options: CAC, fees, and marketable permits.
10. Be able to define and give examples of positive and negative externalities.
11. Be able to define *public good* and the concepts of indivisibility and excludability, and explain how public goods different from private goods.
12. Be able to explain how property rights enter into environmental policy and regulation and to explain the purpose of such actions.

2
Engineering Economics

Microeconomics provided the theory to establish the optimum operating point for any supplier; at the point marginal cost is equal to marginal benefit. However, the costs and benefits which go into such an analysis must first be properly defined. The tool used to define those costs and benefits is engineering economics.

The theory explained in Sec. 1 is based on a snapshot in time. However, it is unlikely that any firm will actually operate at the precise optimal point for an extended period. Hence, in order to use the microeconomic theory, costs and benefits from the future must be expressed in their financial equivalents of the snapshot in time. In this manner, managers can use the estimated marginal costs and benefits to determine the direction their firms must take to become more profitable. Also needed is a way to calculate a value for various revenues and expenses related to different investment options at different times. This task requires its own specific set of tools: engineering economics.

Benefit-Cost Analysis

Benefit-cost analysis is a systematic method of identifying and measuring economic benefits and costs of a project or program. If the analysis is to be used as a decision criterion, for any project or program in which the benefits outweigh the costs, it would be logical that the project or program be undertaken. However, there are two principle limitations in applying this method to environmental situations. First, economic valuation relies on a critical understanding and measurement of the physical, chemical, and biological effects of pollution: an area that is often difficult to quantify. Second, once these effects are known, they must be expressed in constant terms such as monetary values, an exercise which is imperfect and can be politically charged in situations such as putting a price on an increased risk of health effects. These limitations notwithstanding, the concept of benefit-cost analysis holds much promise for environmental managers because it requires a rigorous, systematic analysis of investment possibilities.

Discount Rate

In the environmental arena, costs and benefits often stretch out over decades. Hence, any discussion of environmental costs and/or benefits must begin with a discussion of the time value of money and how that value relates to both the concept of present value and the standard benefit-cost measurement techniques.

All benefit cost measurement techniques rely on the ability to express monies spent or received over time at a present value, i.e., the worth of the future revenues and expenses in terms of today's value. Because of this, the discount rate used by the analyst becomes critical. For example, even at a modest 5 percent discount rate, almost 15 percent of the value of a future payment is lost in just 3 years due to the time value of money (i.e., $1.00 to be received in 3 years is worth only $0.86 in terms of present value). If a firm uses a larger discount rate, the effect of discounting future revenues to present value would be even larger. For example, 15 percent discount rates were common in the late 1970s. At 15 percent, the value of $1.00 in 3 years is reduced to less than $0.66 in present value.

This effect of discount rate leads to dichotomy in selecting the discount rate to be used in the analysis. Everyone wants to earn high interest on their investments, so there is a natural inclination to use the highest possible interest rate in calculating present values. Conversely, especially in the environmental arena, there is a high value placed on the future. This implies that a low discount rate should be used in the analysis. Hence, the "preferred" discount rate depends upon how the analysis is approached. For example, in determining the worth of a giant redwood tree, if one currently owned the tree (e.g., a supplier of fine hardwoods), a high discount rate would be preferred because the value of the asset, the tree, would grow more quickly over time. Conversely, if one were concerned that there may soon be no redwoods left, one would want to place the highest possible value on having the tree in the future; lower discount rates increase the present value of a future asset. Hence, there is a built-in dichotomy in selecting discount rates for environmental projects.

Present Value

The concept of calculating the present value of a future revenue or expense assumes that the rational consumer would both prefer more benefit to less and prefer to receive the benefit now instead of in the future. However, this latter "bird in the hand" preference is driven by emotions in the consumer, and, as such, is typically ignored in a business setting, because firms have no such emotions. Hence, the deciding factor in selecting between investment alternatives is the preference for more versus less.

Mathematically, the relationship between future payments and present value is

$$P = \frac{F}{(1 + r)^n}$$

where P is the present worth or present value of the revenue or expense, F is the actual value of the revenue or expense to be received in the future, r is the interest or discount rate being used, and n is the number of periods under consideration. For example, if a supplier were to receive $1.00 one year in the future and was using a 5 percent interest rate, compounded annually, the computed present value would be

$$P = \frac{\$1.00}{(1 + .05)^1} = \$0.95$$

Because invested money can earn interest or "work," given an interest rate of 5 percent, there is no difference to a firm between receiving $0.95 now or $1.00 in one year because both amounts have the same value in terms of current or present value.

Similarly, if the firm were to receive the $1.00 payment in 3 years, the present value calculation for the payment would be

$$P = \frac{\$1.00}{(1 + .05)^3} = \$0.86$$

Again, the firm would see $0.86 now as financially equivalent to $1.00 in 3 years at a 5 percent discount rate compounded annually.

In the case of multiple payments, either revenues or expenses, or payments both into and out of a firm, the present values of each payment can be added to determine the net result. Referring to the above examples and the 5 percent discount rate used, if the firm were to receive both $1.00 in 1 year and $1.00 in 3 years, the net present value would be $0.95 + $0.86 = $1.81. Similarly, if the firm had the investment opportunity to receive $1.00 in 1 year if it were to pay $1.00 in 3 years, the present value of the investment opportunity would be $0.95 − $0.86 = $.09, the value of the incoming dollar in 1 year less the value of the outgoing dollar in 3 years. Such present worth calculations allow both costs and benefits which are expended or earned in the future to be expressed as a single lump sum at their current or present value. In considering different options, the present value for each option can be computed and compared.

The above examples were specifically chosen to show the future values based on $1.00. This naturally leads to a simplification which can be made in that present values can be computed on a per-dollar basis. As a result, these values can be thought of as factors or multipliers which represent the percentage of worth per dollar of value. As such they can be used in a number of different calculations without repeatedly using the equation over and over. For example, it was shown that $1.00, 3 years in the future, at 5 percent interest compounded annually, was worth $0.86 in present value. If this 0.86 value is then used as a multiplier, then the present value of any revenue or expense, 3 years in the future, at an interest rate of 5 percent, can be calculated. For example, a revenue payment of $1000 would be worth $860, $21,456 would be worth 21,456 × 0.86 = $18,452, and so on. Using such factors allows the time value of money to be expressed quite easily graphically in a plot of present value percentage versus time. Figure 2-1 shows the future worth of $1.00 over time at four interest rates.

The present value factors can be read directly from the graph, and the present value of any amount can be calculated directly. For example, the factor for a 10 percent discount rate, compounded annually, for a payment to be received 15 years in the future, is approximately 0.23. Hence, the present worth of a $30,000 payment to be received 15 years from now would be 0.23 × $30,000 or $6900.

Similarly, the equation for present value can be solved for the future value and used to express the value of a revenue or expense at any time in the future. This allows the analyst to include earned interest over a given number of periods. The equation for future value is

$$F = P(1 + r)^n$$

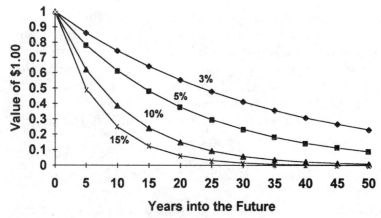

Figure 2-1. The effect of time and interest rate on present value.

with the variables defined as before. Depending upon the situation, either equation can be useful; however, in comparing investment alternatives, because of the dependence on a snapshot in time, all options must be compared at the same point in time: all at present value or all at the same time in the future.

To see how these two equations work, consider lending a friend $10,150 for the purchase of a car. The friend promises to repay $11,000 in 1 year. Assuming the friend to be trustworthy, should the investment be made? The alternative to loaning your friend the money is to take the $10,150 and invest $10,000 in a 1-year certificate of deposit earning 7.5 percent compounded annually (the bank will only accept investments in 1-year certificates in increments of $1000) and invest the remaining $150 in a pass book account earning 4.5 percent annually.

To base the investment opportunity decision on present value, the calculation would be to compare the present value of the capital to be invested ($10,150) to the present value of $11,000 to be received in 1 year. The calculation would be

$$P = \frac{F}{(1 + r)^n} = \frac{\$11,000}{(1 + 0.075)^1} = \$10,232$$

In other words, given the interest rate available for certificates of deposit, the present value of $11,000 received in 1 year is $10,232. Given that this value is greater than the $10,150 to be invested, the investment is financially beneficial and should be made.

However, in this case the calculation assumed that the entire $11,000 could earn 7.5 percent interest. Given the limitations that the bank has placed on investments, it may be more accurate to make the decision based on future value rather than present value. In this case, the decision would be between the future value of $11,000 to be received in 1 year ($11,000) and the future value of $10,150 invested as described above. The calculation for the latter would be

$$F = P(1 + r)^n = \$10,000(1 + 0.075)^1 + \$150(1 + 0.045)^1 = \$10,907$$

Even with the inaccuracy of the present value analysis caused by having to assume the entire amount would earn the higher interest rate, in this case the decision to loan the friend the money does not change; the $11,000 promised in 1 year has a larger future value than the alternative investment ($10,907), so the loan should be made.

From the above discussion it is apparent that the interest rate is a critical factor. However, the interval over which the interest rate is compounded also requires consideration. The interest rate must always be expressed in terms of the compounding interval. This is because of the effect of compounding interest. In other words, if interest is compounded quarterly instead of annually, the investment will grow faster. This is because in the case of quarterly compounding, both the interest earned in the first quarter and the principal will earn interest in the second quarter. Similarly, the interest earned in the first and second quarters as well as the principal will earn interest in the third quarter and so on for the rest of the year.

To show the effect of interval, consider the certificates of deposit shown above and examine the difference in investing $11,000 for 1 year at an interest rate of 7.5 percent compounded quarterly versus annually. The calculation for annual compounding could be

$$F = P(1 + r)^n = \$11,000(1 + 0.075)^1 = \$11,825$$

Conversely, if the interest were compounded quarterly, the quarterly interest rate would be one-quarter the annual rate or 0.25 times 7.5 percent = 1.875 percent quarterly. Hence, the calculation of the future value of the $11,000 investment with quarterly compounding of interest would be

$$F = P(1 + r)^n = \$11,000(1 + 0.01875)^4 = \$11,848$$

The resulting difference, $23, may not seem like a very large sum of money; however, environmental projects in general, and pollution prevention projects specifically, often have revenue and expense flows which can impact the financial decision over many years, and the amounts may be significantly larger than $11,000.

Similarly, if interest is compounded even more often, daily for example, the relatively small difference in the above example can grow. The same equation as shown above would be used to compute the present value until the specific situation of continuous compounding is reached. Then the equation for continuous compounding becomes

$$P = \frac{F}{e^{rn}}$$

where the variables are as previously defined except e, which is a mathematical constant. Table 2-1 shows the effect of the compounding interval on an \$11,000 investment at a 10 percent interest rate.

As can be seen from the table, the "error" incurred in using a discrete compounding interval (e.g., quarterly instead of continuous) is very low, a maximum of -2.3 percent in comparing annual to continuous compounding. Hence, because the mathematics become somewhat more cumbersome in continuous compounding and result in only a small change in the magnitude in the present worth of investment options, it will not be used in this text. In addition, in selecting between investment options, the magnitude of the investment is of less importance than the relative difference between investment options. The critical factor is not generally which investment options have benefit but rather which investment option has the greater benefit. If all options are computed using the same interest rate and period, the relative ranking and investment decision will remain constant. Readers who use spreadsheet software with an e function or who are comfortable with the mathematics can use

Table 2-1. Effect of Compounding Period on Future Value (10 Percent Discount Rate and \$11,000 Investment)

Year	Annual	Quarterly	Monthly	Daily	Continuous
0	\$11,000	\$11,000	\$11,000	\$11,000	\$11,000
1	12,100	12,142	12,152	12,157	12,157
5	17,716	18,025	18,098	18,135	18,136
Error*	-2.37%	-0.62%	-0.21%	-0.01%	0.00%

*Error measured as a difference from continuous compounding.

either discrete or continuous compounding depending upon the specific situation and requirements within their firm or financial institution.

Inflation

When computing future or present values, inflation has the opposite effect of discounting. As shown above, if $0.86 were invested for 3 years at 5 percent interest compounded annually, it would result in a revenue of $0.14 (i.e., $1.00 received less the $0.86 invested). However, if the inflation rate over that same 3-year period were also 5 percent, then the $1.00 received would only have the purchasing power of $0.86 in present value terms. In other words, the $1.00 received 3 years in the future would only be worth $0.86 in today's terms: a net gain of zero.

As with continuous compounding, more complex equations can be used to include the effects of inflation; however, they too can be simplified with little effect on the accuracy of the resulting present value calculations. The specific method to deal with inflation will be demonstrated later in the text.

Benefit-Cost Measures

In the past, justifying environmental projects was largely limited to declaring that if funding weren't awarded, there would be an environmental disaster and lawsuits would follow. Unfortunately, the imprecision of such investment justifications frequently led to many poor decisions in funding pollution prevention projects. Although waste minimization and pollution prevention are always politically sound investments—everyone wants to be connected with producing less pollution—often projects with limited benefit were funded, and in some cases projects which could have had large impacts on profit and cash flow went unfunded. Pollution prevention investment must be approached with the same rigor as any other capital investment available to a supplier; the investments must be able to compete effectively for monies based on the specific financial merits of each individual project.

Unfortunately, this imprecision in representing the worth of pollution prevention projects also leads to these projects being among the first to be postponed in times of budget shortfalls; when resources are in short supply, only the most profitable of investments can be undertaken, and inadequate support and defense of environmental projects on an economic basis leaves them vulnerable. When a production division requests money, all the necessary documentation, facts, and figures are ready for presentation. The production project is justified by showing how the project will increase revenue and how the added revenue will not only recover costs but also increase a company's profits. Pollution prevention project justification requires this same emphasis. To be competitive, an understanding of the financial system is essential to show the importance of the pollution prevention investment on a life cycle or total cost basis: in terms of revenues, expenses, and profits. To predict these impacts, it is critical to understand the financial concepts of life-cycle costing and present worth as well as the basic factors used in making financial decisions.

For most firms, financial decisions are based on one of four benefit-cost measurement techniques: payback period, benefit-cost ratios, internal rate of return, or net present value. In each method, life-cycle costing should be considered.

Life-cycle costing has undergone semantic changes in recent years. For example, in some circles *total cost accounting* is used. However, the basics remain unchanged. *Life-cycle costing,* as used in this text, is a method which analyzes the costs and benefits associated with a piece of equipment or a procedure over the entire time the equipment or procedure is to be used. The concept originated in the federal government and was first applied in procuring weapons systems. Experience showed that the up-front purchase price was a poor measure of the total cost; costs such as those associated with maintainability, reliability, disposal and/or salvage value, and training and/or education had to be given equal weight in the financial decision-making process. Similarly, in justifying pollution prevention investments, all benefits and costs over the entire life of each option must be examined and expressed in the most concrete terms possible.

Comparing Investment Alternatives

Comparing investment alternatives is not complicated once the benefits and costs associated with a project are determined for the entire time the project will be in place. Most often the comparisons are made through one of the following analysis methods.

Payback Period

This method is often used in the research and development arena. Conceptually, the program or project which returns the invested capital most quickly is considered the best investment. The technique for determining payback period again lies in the calculation of present value with two significant exceptions. First, a zero percent interest or discount rate is used. Second, the key variable in the analysis is time rather than present value. The life-cycle costs for the project or program are represented as a single value representing initial or capital cost for the investment. Then the revenues or benefits generated by the investment are summed until the initial costs are recovered. The time it takes to recover the initial investment is referred to as the *payback period.* Ranking projects then becomes a matter of selecting the projects with the shortest payback period.

Often firms will establish a minimum payback standard. For example, investments such as research and development may be required to payback invested capital in 2 years. However, this decision method should be avoided for environmental programs such as pollution prevention because of the two exceptions to the present value equation. The first, and most obvious, is that a zero discount rate is used in all calculations, and this does not accurately represent revenues and expenses which occur in the future. Second, the analysis is designed to stop when the initial investment is recovered. As such, it disregards the lessons learned in life-cycle costing in that it does not take all potential costs into account. Using payback period as a criterion minimizes the impact of long-term expenses and revenues such as potential liability costs. Pollution prevention projects often fall into this long-term category in that these projects are often

Table 2-2. Four Investment Opportunities (3-Year Payback Period)

Year	Option 1	Option 2	Option 3	Option 4
0	($1,000)	($1,000)	($500)	($1,000)
1	400	200	(500)	500
2	400	400	400	500
3	200	400	600	0
4	200	1,000	0	0
5	200	2,000	0	(1,000)
Sum of cash flows	$400	$3,400	$0	($1,000)

"front-loaded" with expenses but can effect savings lasting over years. Given that the analysis is designed to determine the point where the present values of the benefits and costs are equal at a zero discount, front-loaded pollution prevention projects would naturally imply long payback periods. If a competing investment alternative is a project with little up-front costs and large, long-term potential damages (such as sending waste to a landfill), the opposite could be true.

To see how the combination of the low initial costs but high long-term costs could affect the payoff period and ultimately the decision to invest in an option, consider the cash flows from the four investment opportunities shown in Table 2-2. As can be seen in the table, each project will recover all capital costs in 3 years, so under the criteria of payback period, the projects would be nearly equal. However, in looking at the life-cycle costs over the entire 5-year life, it is readily apparent that the projects would not have the same impact on profit. Under the criteria of shortest payback period, the pollution prevention projects with long-term returns may not be undertaken even though they may have the potential to contribute more to profit.

Benefit-Cost Ratio

Benefit-cost ratio is similar to payback period in that the benefits and costs incurred during each period are kept separate; however, this ratio does not require that a zero discount rate be used, and the method includes life-cycle cost considerations in that the benefits and costs over the entire life of the project must be considered. The benefit-cost ratio can be expressed in one of two ways. First, the pure benefit-cost ratio represents the ratio of present value of the project's benefits divided by present value of the project's costs:

$$\text{Benefit-cost ratio} = \frac{\text{present value of benefits}}{\text{present value of costs}}$$

If the resulting ratio is greater than 1.0, the benefits outweigh the costs, and the project is acceptable.

Alternatively, there is the net benefit-cost ratio which is the net benefit (i.e., the present value of the benefits less the present value of the costs) divided by the present value of the costs:

Net benefit-cost ratio =

$$\frac{\text{present value of benefits} - \text{present value of costs}}{\text{present value of costs}}$$

Again, the decision criterion is that the benefits must outweigh the costs, which, in this latter case, implies the net ratio must be greater than zero (e.g., if the benefits exactly equalled the costs, their difference would be zero as would be the net benefit-cost ratio). In both cases, the decision criterion for investment is predicated on the fact that the projects with the highest benefit-cost ratios are the best investment opportunities.

For example, the benefit-cost ratio for option 1 in Table 2-3, would be computed as follows (assuming a 10 percent interest

Table 2-3. Benefit-Cost (B-C) Ratios
for the Four Investments

Option	B-C ratio	Net B-C ratio
1	1.105	0.105
2	2.738	1.738
3	0.817	−0.182
4	0.535	−0.553

rate, compounded annually, and payments made at the end of the period). The present value of the costs is

$$PV_{cost} = \frac{\$1000}{(1 + 0.10)^0} = \$1000$$

Similarly, the present value of the benefits would be

$$\frac{\$400}{(1 + 0.10)^1} + \frac{\$400}{(1 + 0.10)^2} + \frac{\$200}{(1 + 0.1)^3} + \frac{\$200}{(1 + 0.10)^4} + \frac{\$200}{(1 + 0.1)^5}$$
$$= \$1105$$

This results in a benefit-cost ratio of

$$\text{Benefit-cost ratio} = \frac{\$1105}{\$1000} = 1.105$$

or a net benefit-cost ratio of

$$\text{Net benefit-cost ratio} = \frac{\$1105 - \$1000}{\$1000} = 0.105$$

If similar calculations were performed on the other three investment options shown in Table 2-2, the benefit-cost ratios for the four investment opportunities would be as displayed in Table 2-3. As shown in the table, the projects can no longer be considered financially equal.

Using the benefit-cost ratio is clearly superior to payback period in selecting between investment options because the ratio takes both the time value of money and the life-cycle costs into account. However, there is the inherent problem in that the method requires that interest and inflation rates be preselected. In addition, because this method relies on expressing the worth of a project as a ratio, there is a potential for overstating the project "value." For example, assume a firm was to consider a project with a present value of the benefits of $100 and the present value of the costs of $60. Clearly, the benefit-cost ratio would be $100/$60 or 1.67—net benefit-cost ratio would be ($100 − $60)/$60 = 0.67. However, what would happen if the proponent of the project reviewed the analysis and determined that some of the costs of the project could be dealt with as offsetting expenses. Under this assumption the benefit-cost ratio could be changed considerably. For example, if it was determined that $50 of the $60 total cost was due to waste disposal charges, and $70 of the $100 benefit was because the new technology minimized waste volume, thereby avoiding waste disposal costs, the proponent could logically justify the use of offsetting the cost of waste disposal charges to the benefit of not generating waste. The results of this offset, because the method uses a ratio, would be that both the numerator and denominator would be reduced by $50 with the following effect: ($100 − $50)/($60 − $50) = 5.0. Hence, without changing the project, the new benefit-cost ratio would make the project seem to be considerably better. This implies that great care must be taken to keep the benefits and costs separate before computing present values.

Internal Rate of Return

Again, this method is based on the net present value of benefits and costs; however, it does not use a predetermined discount rate. Instead, the discount rate is left as the variable, and the present value equations for the cost are set equal to the present value equations for the benefits. Computationally, it requires simultaneously solving the present value equations for all costs and benefits over the life of the project. The resulting discount rate represents the actual return on the investment over the life of the project. In other words, the method determines what discount rate would result in a net present value of zero given the stream of benefits and costs over time. The discount rate that satisfies the zero benefit is the rate of return on the investment. Project selection is then based on selecting those projects with the highest rate of return with most firms often setting some minimum acceptable value. If the calculations were performed on the above four investment options, the returns on investment would be as shown in Table 2-4.

As shown by the benefit-cost ratio analysis, the projects are clearly not equivalent. From a return on investment standpoint, investing in option 2 would be the equivalent to a bank saving account drawing nearly 45 percent interest.

Although this method is frequently used in business, there are

Table 2-4. Rates of Return on
the Four Investments

Option	Rate of return
1	14.75%
2	44.90
3	0.02
4	0.03

two difficulties. First, since the net benefits and costs during each time period must be separately established, computationally it could be cumbersome in that it could require dealing with a large number of simultaneous equations. Second, in a theoretical sense, the mathematics behind the method make the assumption that the benefits received over the life of the project are reinvested, which may or may not actually occur in practice. Conversely, unlike the other methods, internal rate of return [also referred to as rate of return (ROR) or return on investment (ROI)] does not require that a preselected interest rate be used in the computation.

Net Present Value

This evaluation technique requires that all benefits and costs to be received or expended be determined and evaluated at their current or present values. The decision criterion used is that the projects with the greatest present value are the most beneficial for the firm. Theoretically, any time the net present value (present value of the benefits less the present value of the costs) is greater than zero, the project is worth undertaking in that it will increase the profit of the firm. In cases where the net is less than zero, then the costs outweigh the benefits, and the project should be abandoned. Assuming a 10 percent interest rate compounded annually, the net present values for the four options would be as shown in Table 2-5.

As before, the worth of the investment options in terms of profit are clear from the net present value analysis. The compu-

Table 2-5. Net Present Values
for the Four Investments

Option	Net present value
1	$105
2	1,738
3	(173)
4	(132)

tations indicate that selecting option 2 would be the equivalent of adding a $1738 revenue to the firm.

Although this technique is firmly grounded in microeconomic theory, it has the innate and unavoidable problem that it forces the project proponent to either select interest rates, inflation rates, and so on or use standard values dictated by the firm. As a result, long-term benefits could be under- or overstated. However, given that each option will be examined using the same variables of interest, inflation factors, and so on the same error is imposed on each option. In this manner, the accuracy of the relative rankings of each project is consistent. With respect to the actual ranking of investment options, those with the highest net present value should be funded and implemented first. Because of the problems indicated with the other methods and the computational simplicity of net present value, this method is preferred for pollution prevention project evaluation.

**Selecting Investment
Opportunities**

There must be a margin of safety when using any of the above selection criteria. If the preferred method, net present value, were used, the theory states that any project with a positive net value should be pursued. However, this criterion assumes that the analysis will accurately reflect reality once the project has been initiated. For example, consider the simple investment analysis between leasing or purchasing an automobile. Such an analysis would contain a number of variables to predict: interest rate, inflation rate, maintenance costs, insurance premiums, and so on. In each case, the present value analysis treats these variables as reality; however, what if the price of gasoline were to rise greatly such as during Operation Desert Storm? What if the insurance rates were to increase faster than predicted? Even in this simple case where the two options both involved using an automobile, the actual return on the investment could vary considerably. In more complex situations which involve equipment purchase and maintenance, labor, utilities, and so on for a number of dissimilar options, this uncertainty could completely alter the analysis.

In financial analysis, uncertainty can be handled in two ways. First, each cost and benefit variable can be treated as a range of values from the best and worst cases. For example, gasoline costs can be estimated at a worst case of 16 miles per gallon and $1.20 per gallon and a best case of 20 miles per gallon and $0.95 per gallon. In this case, two separate financial analyses would be performed showing the net present value under each condition. If the net present value were positive under the worst case, then the investment should be safe. Alternately, if the net present value were negative under the worst case, but positive under the best case, a judgment would have to be made based on the firm's willingness to accept risk.

Alternatively, the analysis can be performed once with a safety margin applied to the resulting "best guess" net present value. For example, once the rack and stack of projects from the highest to the lowest net present value is done, a criterion reflecting the uncertainty in the analysis can be applied. For example, in simple projects with few variables, one might eliminate any project whose net present value is not at least 10 percent of the invested capital. Similarly, for more complex investments with a larger number of variables, this minimum percentage may be increased. The same method can be used to deal with different types of projects such as research and development, which would require a relatively large margin of safety, versus capital investment projects, which would require a smaller margin of safety.

This minimally acceptable return is similar to the approach that is used by suppliers who base financial decisions on return-on-investment criteria. Normally, some type of minimal percentage or hurdle rate is applied in the decision process. In this case, the investment opportunities are again ranked from greatest to least return on investment and then a hurdle rate is applied, with projects whose return is less than this minimal return eliminated from consideration.

No matter which investment criterion is used, a method to allow for the uncertainty in the analysis must be included when the final selection is made.

Conclusions

Businesses, like consumers, are faced with the simple fact that there will never be enough money to do it all. The problem of a finite amount of resources and an infinite demand are normal, and each investment proponent must fight for its "share of the pie." Although the cost-benefit analyses shown above are among the best techniques to select among investment opportunities, they are not without problems. As indicated earlier, even the seemingly simple task of selecting an interest or discount rate for use in present value computations could alter the financial outcome.

Conversely, cost-benefit analysis has proven to be an important disciplinary ingredient in performing investment decisions from two standpoints. First, it establishes a consistent framework for uniform project evaluations. Second, especially in the environmental arena, it has forced financial discipline into what was often a political process. It is critically important to include ex post (i.e., after the fact) analyses of projects to enable analysts to compare projected and actual results of investments. In this manner, more and more of the guesswork can be removed and predictive abilities improved.

Case Study: A Simple Case of Capital Investment

Estimating the benefit of pollution prevention investment relies on the ability of the proponent to show the cost of business as usual versus the cost of the pollution prevention investment alternatives. As a result, the seven steps in the financial analysis are

- Determine investment alternatives (including business as usual.
- Determine the variables to be included in the analysis.
- Determine the revenues and/or expenses.
- Establish the required equations.
- Compute the net present value, return on investment, payback period, and so on as required by the firm.
- Rank-order the investment alternatives.
- Apply minimum acceptable criterion to eliminate projects with unacceptable returns.

For this example, assume that a firm spends $1250 per month to dispose of waste solvent from its part-washing operation. After investigation, it is discovered that a new piece of equipment is available which uses a nonhazardous solvent which would eliminate the hazardous waste disposal costs. Hence, this example involves only two investment alternatives: business as usual or purchasing the new, nonhazardous solvent equipment.

The variables in the analysis would be the interest rate, inflation, cost of waste disposal, operating and maintenance on the equipment, utilities, labor, and so on; however, to keep this first analysis simple, it shall be assumed that all variables for the two operations are the same except for waste disposal and equipment cost (e.g., the same labor, utilities, and so on are required for either operation). In addition, inflation can be eliminated because in this example, the firm was lucky enough to lock in a long-term contract guaranteeing the cost of waste disposal. Further, no changes in production are expected over the life of the equipment, so waste volume will be constant.

In determining the revenues-expenses (or benefits-costs), it shall be assumed that under the first alternative, purchase of the new part washer, the equipment cost is $65,000, but the waste disposal cost be would be completely eliminated. Conversely, the business as usual alternative would require that $15,000 per year (i.e., $1250/month × 12 months/year) be spent on waste disposal. If the equipment were expected to last 5 years, the two investment alternatives could be represented as follows:

Expenses during year	Option 1: Business as usual	Option 2: Pollution prevention
1	$15,000	$65,000
2	15,000	0
3	15,000	0
4	15,000	0
5	15,000	0
Total	$75,000	$65,000

For simplicity, these revenues and expenses are normally shown graphically on a time line. The time line is established from time "0" through the life of the project (5 years in this case). The revenues and expenses are then summed during each accounting period, and the totals are represented by arrows or bars with revenues shown up and expenses down. The revenues and expenses for the business as usual option would be as shown in Fig. 2-2. Similarly, the pollution prevention option would be a single down bar at time 0 representing the $65,000 investment.

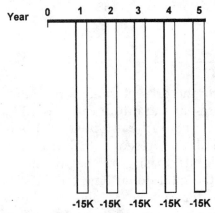

Figure 2-2. Revenues and expenses for the business-as-usual option.

Using Net Present Value

At first glance, the pollution prevention option would seem the alternative of choice, an expenditure of $65,000 versus $75,000; however, the analysis requires that all costs must be compared at the same point in time—"apples to apples." As such, the annual waste disposal expenses must be represented at a single point in time using the present value equations before they can be compared to the $65,000 investment. As shown earlier, all values can be expressed in the future, present, or at any time, and the investment decision will be the same. In this case, since the present value of the pollution prevention option is known, it is computationally easier to compute the annual waste disposal payments in present value. The equations then would be those for the present value of a future payment, shown earlier, with a separate calculation being performed for each annual payment.

The computations, using the present value equation with 6 percent interest compounded annually, for the business as usual option would result in the following:

Year	Option 1: Business as usual	Present value
1	$15,000	$14,150
2	15,000	13,350
3	15,000	12,595
4	15,000	11,881
5	15,000	11,209
Total	$75,000	$63,185

As an alternative to calculating the present value formula for each year, a table showing the present and future values of $1.00 at the firm's current interest rate could be established. Then, because the table has computed all the present value factors for a $1.00 payment (i.e., on a per-dollar basis), all that would be required would be to multiply the total dollar amount ($15,000 above) by the appropriate factor for each year. Table 2-6 shows both the present value factors for a future payment of $1.00 at the selected 6 percent interest rate.

Table 2-6. Present Value Factors for 6 Percent
Interest Rate Compounded Annually

Year	Factor
1	0.943396
2	0.889996
3	0.839619
4	0.792094
5	0.747258
6	0.704961
7	0.665057
8	0.627412
9	0.591898
10	0.558395

In this example, the present value is required, and the future
payment is stated, so simply multiplying the factor from the second column by the amount of the payment is the only computation that need be made. Further, since all five payments are
equal, the following simplifications can be made:

$$PV = \sum (\$15,000 \times PV_{yri})$$

which can be rewritten as

$$PV = (\$15,000) \sum (PV_{yri})$$

As a result, all that needs to be done is to add the present value
factors for years 1 through 5 and multiply the result by $15,000.

$$PV = \$15,000 \,(4.212363) = \$63,185$$

The result is identical to that calculated by computing each individual equation.

As a result of the present value analysis, the pollution prevention
investment (present value = $65,000) was shown to be more costly
than the annual waste disposal costs (present value = $63,185).

In rank-ordering alternatives, the first consideration is the number of significant figures. Although Table 2-6 contains seven significant figures, the actual present value, given the uncertainty in the variables, is generally much less accurate, and generally only two or three significant figures should be used. In this case, the present value of the waste disposal option should be shown as either $63,000 or $63,200, and the ranking of the alternatives does not change. Selecting the business as usual option is the financial equivalent to spending $63,000 versus spending $65,000 for the pollution prevention option. Hence, in this simplified example, the pollution prevention investment should not be undertaken, and the firm should continue to dispose of the waste.

Using Return on Investment

Under the criterion of return on investment, a similar set of equations is used; however, the interest rate becomes the variable of interest. The interest rate required to make the present value cost of the pollution prevention investment equal to the present value of continued waste disposal is the business as usual option. The present value equations for the business as usual option (PV_{BAU}) would be

$$PV_{BAU} = \frac{\$15,000}{(1+r)^1} + \frac{\$15,000}{(1+r)^2} + \frac{\$15,000}{(1+r)^3} + \frac{\$15,000}{(1+r)^4} + \frac{\$15,000}{(1+r)^5}$$

Similarly, the present value of the pollution prevention option (PV_{PP}) would be represented as the present value of a $65,000 payment received 0 years in the future:

$$PV_{PP} = \frac{\$65,000}{(1+r)^0}$$

Since the desired outcome is the breakeven interest rate, the present value equations for the two options are set equal and then solved for the interest rate.

Iterating to solve for the interest rate, r, yields a value of just over 5 percent. This means that the investment option would yield a rate of return of approximately 5 percent. If a firm could get a 6 percent return on its monies in a certificate of deposit or fund account of some sort, its hurdle rate would be set at least at that level. Hence, as before, the pollution prevention option would not be pursued. Conversely, if the firm's hurdle rate were to fall to below 5 percent, the pollution prevention option would be economically attractive.

One additional consideration is that of the interest period. As shown in Table 2-1, although the differences are relatively small between annual and continuous compounding (on the order of 2 percent), it is a worthwhile exercise to compute the changes for this example. If the above investments were analyzed based on monthly compounding of interest (as was practiced by credit card companies) instead of annual compounding, would the investment decision be altered? In this case, there would be 60 periods [i.e., (12 months/years) × (5 years)] and the interest rate would be 0.5 percent [i.e., (6 percent/year)/(12 months/year)]. Again, to simplify the computations, a present value table could be established as done in Table 2-7.

Table 2-7. Present Value Factors for 6 Percent Interest Rate Compounded Monthly

Month	Factor
1	0.995025
2	0.990075
3	0.985149
4	0.980248
5	0.975371
6	0.970518
7	0.96569
8	0.960885
9	0.956105
10	0.951348
11	0.946615
12	0.941905
24	0.887186
36	0.835645
48	0.787098
60	0.741372

If the computations are performed with a 0.5 percent interest table, the result is that the present value cost of waste disposal is $62,898! In other words, monthly compounding would save approximately $700 (roughly 1 percent of the capital investment) as compared to annual compounding. However, the pollution prevention investment decision would not change.

In deciding between more complex investments, the computations become more laborious, but the procedure is the same. All that is needed is to simply work through the seven steps outlined earlier. Alternatively, in simple cases the revenues and expenses for business as usual and the investment options could be shown on the same time line. In this case, the revenues (benefits) of making the investment would be the costs from the business as usual option which were avoided. For the pollution prevention investment opportunity discussed above, this combined time line would be as shown in Fig. 2-3. In this case, the revenues and expenses become more apparent. The decision becomes whether to accept the $65,000 initial investment if it is offset by five annual payments of $15,000. The equation for present value would be

$$PV = -\frac{\$65{,}000}{(1 + 0.06)^0} + \frac{\$15{,}000}{(1 + 0.06)^1} + \frac{\$15{,}000}{(1 + 0.06)^2} + \frac{\$15{,}000}{(1 + 0.06)^3} +$$

$$\frac{\$15{,}000}{(1 + 0.06)^4} + \frac{\$15{,}000}{(1 + 0.06)^5}$$

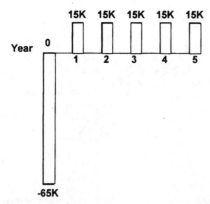

Figure 2-3. Combining benefits and costs on a single revenue-expense time line.

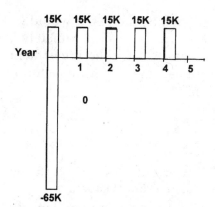

Figure 2-4. Revenues and expenses realized at the beginning of each accounting period.

Solving the equation for PV would result in the same answer as subtracting the present values for the business as usual and pollution prevention options: approximately −$2000.

Displaying revenues and expenses in this manner also shows an additional important factor. The assumption made in this example is that the payments would occur at the end of the year. However, given the assumption that we had signed an agreement guaranteeing the cost of disposal, it would not be unusual for the disposal contractor to insist on payments at the beginning of the year rather than at the end. In this case, the revenue-expense time line would be as shown in Fig. 2-4. The new present value equation resulting from this change in payment time would be

$$PV = -\frac{\$65,000}{(1 + 0.06)^0} + \frac{\$15,000}{(1 + 0.06)^0} + \frac{\$15,000}{(1 + 0.06)^1} + \frac{\$15,000}{(1 + 0.06)^2} +$$

$$\frac{\$15,000}{(1 + 0.06)^3} + \frac{\$15,000}{(1 + 0.06)^4}$$

Solving the equation for the PV of the project would indicate a $2000 revenue instead of the $2000 expense. The difference is due to the fact that if the savings can be taken at the beginning of a period, the monies can earn interest during that period. Likewise, if the computations for return on investment were redone for beginning-of-the-year payments, the result would be an increase in the return from investment from approximately 5 to 7.7 percent, a change that could easily alter the investment decision. Hence, the time of payment becomes a critical factor in selecting between investment options.

Study Concepts

1. Be able to discuss the "conflict" between the desire for high and low interest rates in an environmental investment situation.

2. Be able to describe the following and comment on their strengths and weaknesses with respect to investment justification: (*a*) net present value of benefits; (*b*) payback period; (*c*) benefit-cost ratio; (*d*) internal rate of return.

3. Given any stream of benefits and/or costs be able to compute net present value.

4. Be able to show how the date of payment can affect the analysis of present worth.

5. Be able to discuss the effects on present value of (*a*) changing interest rates; (*b*) changing the computation period; (*c*) inflation.

3

Accounting Principles

Microeconomics determined the point at which a company should operate (i.e., marginal cost equal to marginal revenue) and, in turn, whether an investment would be worthwhile on an economic basis. Next, engineering economics provided the tools required to measure and compare the revenues and expenses in terms of present or future values. However, unless the costs and benefits can be categorized, both the microeconomic theory and the tools are of little use. To clarify expenses and revenues, accounting becomes a critical bookkeeping tool in the financial analysis of pollution prevention investment.

In categorizing the revenues and expenses throughout this section, it will become apparent that the definition of cost or benefit depends on how the situation is examined in much the same manner as the Redwood tree example presented earlier. Often the "benefit" of a project must be defined as the avoided cost made possible by the change. This approach eliminates the confusion of having only cost comparisons upon which to determine the attractiveness of an investment and allows the use of time lines to show two investment opportunities simultaneously.

For example, assume a company spends $X on a process in its everyday business. The company then discovers that it could "improve" the process by implementing a new procedure at a cost of $Y; should it make the investment? In analyzing the investment option, instead of comparing the two costs ($X versus $Y) and selecting the lower cost, the cost of doing business as usual is taken as a benefit of implementing the new procedure, i.e., the benefit of the new procedure is the avoidance of the business as usual costs. Hence, the critical value is the difference in the two costs ($X − $Y) of the net present value if the new procedure were to be implemented. A negative difference means that the new procedure costs more than the old (i.e., $Y > $X) and should not be implemented.

Basic Accounting Concepts

Two basic equations in accounting are helpful for our purposes—one is an expression of the worth of a firm, the accounting equation, and the other expresses its profit, the profit equation. Both become critical in the analysis of investment options.

The Accounting Equation

The accounting equation starts with a measure of a company's tangible and intangible assets: land, buildings, cars and trucks, equipment, patents, copyrights, and so on—everything of worth owned by the company. Since the company itself has owners, private parties, partnerships, stockholders, taxpayers, and so on, this worth ultimately belongs to the owners and is referred to as *equity*. Unfortunately, this equity can be positive or negative, for it is not only the owners who have a stake in the company's assets; creditors must also be included. For example, if a company purchases a new car with a loan from the bank, the part of the car represented by the down payment belongs to the purchaser, and the part of the car represented by the promissory note belongs to the bank. Hence, the owner's true equity, referring to the "owner" as the owner of the company, is the firm's assets less the firm's liabilities. This simple statement of the economic worth of a company, dubbed the *accounting equation*, is shown below and forms the critical relationship for the purposes of accounting for revenues and expenses:

$$\text{Assets} - \text{liabilities} = \text{owner's equity}$$

As will be seen in the discussion of opportunity cost, the key aspect of the accounting equation is that if one asset (e.g., cash) is traded for another asset (e.g., equipment), the owner's equity is not affected by the transaction even though there was an expenditure.

The Profit Equation

The second equation of concern in accounting for revenues and expenses is the profit equation. Simply stated, if revenues are larger than expenses, profit has been made:

$$\text{Revenues} - \text{expenses} = \text{profit}$$

In general, there are two definitions of profit. In the accounting arena, any time revenues exceed expenses it is considered profit. Conversely, to an economist, before there can be profit, there must be a return on the invested capital. This can be most easily clarified by an example. If a car manufacturer built a new plant which resulted in revenues of $500 million, at a cost of $490 million, there would be accounting profit of $10 million: $500 million − $490 million = $10 million. Conversely, if the manufacturer had a minimum hurdle rate of 10 percent (representing the earning potential for investments in certificates of deposit and the like), the $490 million had the potential to earn $49 million with complete safety in a bank. Hence, the economist would include this figure into the equation, and the investment in the new plant would be perceived as a lose of $39 million. This concept is similar to a minimum hurdle rate when using the investment criteria of internal rate of return or setting a minimum percentage of return on investment to select between investment options as discussed in the previous section.

The critical aspect of the profit equation that often seems to be overlooked in the environmental arena is that a firm does not have to increase revenue to increase profit. Decreasing expenses has the same effect as raising revenues, and therein lies the selling power of pollution prevention. Even though it is rare to increase revenues in environmental projects such as pollution prevention, profit can nevertheless be affected by reduced expenses.

In cases where profit is not an issue, such as with federal and state government agencies, the three elements of the profit equation have an even bigger impact. In such agencies, instead of making a profit, the concern is to break even. Hence, the right side of the profit equation is automatically set to zero and the goal of the firm becomes one of matching revenues to expenses. Given that revenue is generally fixed by the budget during any given accounting period, there is very little control over that element. As a result, expenses are the only variable that can be influenced. Given the zero profit constraint, decreasing expenses has the same effect of increasing revenues. Hence, the profit analysis is even more critical in nonprofit agencies in that it clearly shows that expense is the only controllable variable that can increase revenue. As a result, expenses are the critical element in performing pollution prevention investment analyses.

Defining a Project's Cost— the Baseline

As shown in the examples in the previous section, there are seven steps in conducting a financial analysis. Determining the investment alternatives, step 1, begins with establishing baseline costs. The next four steps, determining the variables for the analysis, determining the revenues and expenses, setting up the equations, and computing the variable of interest (e.g., net present value) are then performed for the baseline and each alternative. The final two steps, rank ordering the alternatives and eliminating unacceptable alternatives, are performed after the variable of interest has been determined for all alternatives. This baseline cost calculation forms the comparative basis to which all other alternatives are compared.

Under the assumption that the company is currently in compliance with all applicable environmental regulations, the "do-nothing" or "status quo" alternative is generally used as a baseline. Then, because of the simplifications available when using net present value, any changes in material use, utility expense, and so on for other options being considered are measured as either more or less expensive than the baseline. These "deltas" then are used to calculate the net benefits and costs of the investment alternatives.

Determining the Variables

McHugh (1990) outlines four tiers of potential costs-benefits which have to be examined in investigating pollution prevention investments:

- Tier 0: Usual costs such as direct labor, materials, equipment, and so on
- Tier 1: Hidden costs such as monitoring expenses, reporting, and record keeping, and permit requirements
- Tier 2: Future liability costs such as remedial actions, personal injury under the Occupational Safety and Health Act (OSHA), property damage, and so on
- Tier 3: Less tangible costs such as consumer response, employee relations, and corporate image

McHugh's tier 0 and tier 1 costs are the more obvious costs which would include the engineering, materials, labor, construction, contingency, and so on as well as operation and maintenance costs such as waste collection and transportation services, raw material consumption (increase or decrease), and production costs. Conversely, his tier 2 and tier 3 costs represent intangible expenses and revenues. As such, they are much more difficult to define and include possible expenses such as potential corrective actions under the Resource Conservation and Recovery Act (RCRA), possible site remediation at third-party sites under Superfund, liabilities that could arising from third-party lawsuits for personal and/or property damages, and benefits of improved safety and work environments. Although these intangible costs are frequently more difficult to predict accurately, in terms of impact, they can be the most important. To this end, there is a considerable amount of ongoing research, including the case study addressing long-term liability from landfilling hazardous waste which will be presented later.

When analyzing the financial impact of investment alternatives, it is often useful to further categorize the tier 0 and tier 1 costs as either procurement costs or operations costs, since both these cost categories are normally easy to delineate when collecting cost data from equipment manufactures. Procurement costs are of shorter duration and refer to all costs required to bring a new piece of equipment or a new procedure on line. Conversely, operations costs are long term and represent all costs of operating the equipment or performing the procedure in the post procurement phase.

Determining the Revenues-Expenses

For illustrative purposes, the do-nothing or status quo baseline option shall be examined using a hypothetical, small electronics firm. This firm cleans circuit boards with a chlorinated solvent as one step in its manufacturing process. Because the solvent is hazardous, the wastewater from rinsing the boards is defined under the Resource Conservation and Recovery Act (RCRA) as a hazardous waste. The company is considering pollution prevention options which will reduce the volume of hazardous waste generated over the next 10 years. In establishing the baseline, using the hazardous solvent is the status quo option and therefore, there are no procurement expenses and the analysis will center around operating costs.

The simplest way to establish the baseline costs and benefits to be considered in the analysis is to add up the relevant input and output materials for the process and then compute their appropriate dollar value. This is done by diagraming the operation and performing a mass balance of materials entering and leaving the operation which contribute to cost, in this case, the waste. Figure 3-1 shows a mass balance diagram for a typical solvent rinse tank in the hypothetical firm.

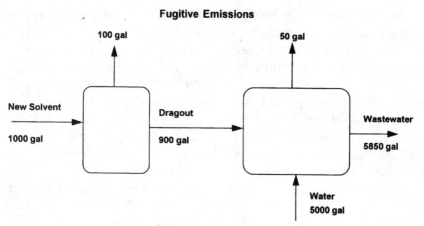

Figure 3-1. Material balance for the hazardous solvent.

After the material balance is accomplished, the first check that must be made is one of common sense, i.e., the entire mass of the solvent purchased must be accounted for in the losses, product, and/or waste. In the example shown above, the solvent purchased (or net change in inventory) must be balanced with that which is lost to evaporation in the cleaning tank and in the waste rinse water from dragout on the pieces taken out of the solvent bath. Once accomplished, determining the baseline cost for the solvent becomes a simple matter of pricing each input and output variable and multiplying their volumes or masses by the appropriate unit cost and then multiplying by the total number of tanks in the firm. For simplicity, the small electronics firm will have only one tank. The baseline costs for the example are shown in Table 3-1.

Table 3-1. Current Costs for Circuit Board Cleaning

Item	Cost/gallon	Gallons/year	Cost/year
Solvent	$3.25	1,000	$3,250
Water	$2.10/1000	5,000	$10.50
Waste disposal	$2.50	5,850	$14,625
Total annual cost			$17,885.50

The next step would be to examine expected business changes such as business expansions, new accounts, rising prices, and so on over the period in question as these could lead to changes in the mass balance diagram of solvent used in the process; if the company's business was expected to increase by 10 percent per year over the time period, the solvent mass balance would have to be adjusted accordingly. For simplicity, the Table 3-1 costs and volumes will be assumed constant. This means that the current annual costs will be the same in the out-years except for one very important aspect, the time value of money.

Given the assumptions made regarding constant cost, constant usage, and no inflation, the annual cost, $17,885 shown in Table 3-1, will be constant over each year for the 10-year analysis. The present value calculations shown in previous chapters enable these future expenditures to be expressed as a single sum which includes the time value of money. The first year's cost, assuming the bills were paid at the end of the year, would be the amount of money that the firm would save, starting today, to pay a $17,885 bill in one year. Computationally, using a 10 percent interest rate and the Sec. 2 formulas, the calculation would be as follows:

$$PV = \frac{F}{(1 + r)^n} = \frac{\$17,885}{(1 + 0.10)^1} = \$16,260$$

This means if $16,260 were banked at 10 percent interest, it would provide enough monies to pay the $17,885 bill at the end of the year. Similarly, the second, third, fourth, and so on years' expenditures (step 5) can also be expressed in present value terms. The results of these computations are displayed in Table 3-2.

The analysis indicates that the total cost of the cleaning system under the business as usual option, over the next 10 years, given a 10 percent interest rate, is $109,896 in present value terms. In other words, considering the earlier discussion regarding significant figures, if $110,000 were invested today at 10 percent interest, there would be sufficient funds available to pay the entire water and wastewater costs for the circuit board cleaning operation for the next 10 years. Hence, any changes to the operation of the firm can now be compared to this $110,000 baseline. Any change which would result in a lower 10-year cost would be a benefit in that it would save money; any option with

Table 3-2. Present Value Calculations
for the Electronics Firm

Year	Expenditure	Present value
1	$17,885	$16,259
2	17,885	14,781
3	17,885	13,437
4	17,885	12,216
5	17,885	11,105
6	17,885	10,096
7	17,885	9,178
8	17,885	8,343
9	17,885	7,585
10	17,885	6,895
Total		$109,896

a higher present value cost will be more expensive and should not be adopted from a financial or economic standpoint.

Although it may seem that a number of potential costs (e.g., utilities, labor) have been ignored, this first step was only meant to establish a baseline. As a result of opting to use net present value, expenses and revenues can be expressed more easily as changes from this baseline. For example, if the current, status quo system uses $100/year in electricity and one of the options being considered would decrease this to $50/year, it is simpler to show the $50 savings as a $50 benefit or revenue rather than to compute both costs individually.

Initial pollution prevention efforts often require little more financial justification than the savings related to tier 0 or possibly tier 1 costs. However, as a firm gets more sophisticated with subsequent pollution prevention efforts, the less tangible tier 2 and 3 costs will become more important. Even if these costs cannot be accurately predicted, recognizing that they exist can still be valuable in the decision phase of the analysis. For example, in cases where two investment options appear to be financially equivalent, if one is a pollution prevention project, tier 2 and 3 considerations such as potential liability or customer reaction to the "greening" of the firm, even if not expressed as present value monies, can favor the pollution prevention investment.

Revenues

Revenue is money coming into the firm, from sale of goods or services, rental fees, interest income, and so on. From the profit equation, it can be seen that revenue increases lead to direct increases in profit and vice versa if all expenses are held constant.

In investigating revenues from investing in pollution prevention, the only consideration that generally needs be made is the case where a saleable byproduct is either generated or eliminated if the pollution prevention project is implemented. For example, if a firm had been generating revenue from selling the fly-ash from burning coal in the boilers and it were to switch to natural gas to cut down on air emissions, it would have a decrease in revenue from the fly ash sales which should be considered in the analysis. Conversely, if a firm generated hazardous sludge which could be sold if it were not for the hazardous metal content, changing the manufacturing procedures to eliminate the hazardous metals would result in a saleable byproduct, and the revenues generated would be considered in the economic analysis for the pollution prevention option.

At this point, only strict revenues, instead of including expenditures which were avoided, are considered in the analysis. For example, if a firm was investigating a process change such as moving from liquid to dry paint stripping as a method to reduce water consumption, although it is true that in the overall analysis the savings resulting from reduced water consumption would be shown as revenue and would affect profit, such a change is expense centered and would not be considered during the revenue analysis. Since expense-centered changes, such as shortened cleanup time from dry paint stripping operations (such as bead blasting) or the elimination of the liquid hazardous waste stream are changes to the baseline expenses, these differences will be considered as expense reductions which, as shown in the profit equation, will also add to the firm's profit. Hence, only changes in the generation of marketable byproducts need be considered under this step of the analysis.

Expenses

Expenses are monies leaving the firm to cover the costs of operations, maintenance, insurance, and so on. Although many costs are specific to individual pollution prevention options (e.g., different pieces of equipment have unique maintenance requirements), there are a number of common cost considerations. The following is a summary of the major cost categories for pollution prevention investment and the potential effects they can have on expenses.

Insurance Expense

Depending upon the specific pollution prevention project, insurance expense could either increase or decrease. For example, OSHA has set exposure limits for workers who must handle a number of chlorinated solvents. If one pollution prevention option were to eliminate a hazardous, chlorinated solvent from production operations, there could be savings in employee health coverage, liability insurance, and so on. Likewise, using a nonflammable solvent in place of a flammable one could lead to a decrease in the fire insurance premium.

Conversely, insurance expense could be increased. For example, if a still were added to a process operation to recover a solvent by distillation, fire insurance premiums could increase. Depending upon the premium change (if any), expenses, and in turn profits, could be increased or decreased by pollution prevention investment and must be included in the analysis.

Although it may not be readily apparent, no endeavors do not have insurance expense. Although many concerns, such as the federal government, may not directly purchase insurance from an outside agent, they still have insurance expense. If a firm has sufficient assets to cover losses, it simply means that it is self-insured, an option available to nearly any private entrepreneur.

If a pollution prevention investment eliminates a hazardous situation, thereby lowering employee and public risk, it is only sensible to include that lowered risk as a reduced cost in the analysis. In cases where the company is self-insured, the projected change in insurance rates quoted from an outside carrier would be a good estimate of the benefit.

Interest Expense

Pollution prevention, like any other investment, implies one of two things must occur; either a firm must fund the project from its own cash reserve or it must finance the cost by borrowing money from a bank, issuing bonds, and so on. If a firm pays for a pollution prevention project out of its own cash reserves, there is obviously no interest expense. However, the expenditure of funds does represent an opportunity cost, since funds used for the investment are unavailable for other expenditures; this consideration will be addressed later in this section.

Conversely, if cash for the investment must be borrowed, there is an interest charge connected with using someone else's money. Interest is a true expense and must be treated as an offset to the project's benefits as would any other expenditure connected with the project such as maintenance requirements, capital costs, and so on. The magnitude of the expense will vary with bank lending rates, returns paid on corporate notes issued, and the like and can readily be computed for each period during the life of the project.

Human Resources Expense

In most cases, the firm's human resources requirements will change due to implementing the pollution prevention project. As pointed out in the dry paint stripping example, the effect could be positive, a decrease in production time, or, if extra worker-hours were required to run new equipment, perform preventive maintenance, and so on, the effect could be an increase in production time and, in turn, human resources expenses.

When computing expenses in this category, the tier 1 expenses can also play an important role. For example, assume a material substitution project eliminated a hazardous input material which, in turn, eliminated a hazardous waste. The elimination of the waste could imply a significant decrease in worker-hours required to complete and track RCRA hazardous waste manifests, label hazardous waste containers, handle and store hazardous waste drums, and so on. This implies that both direct, tier 0, expenses (e.g., 2 hours per week preventive maintenance on the pollution prevention equipment) and secondary, tier 1, expenses can affect costs for workers. However, care must be taken in investigating the effect on tier 1 costs. For example, a firm may have an employee devoted to tracking hazardous waste manifests, doing waste storage area inspections, and so on. However, unless the pollution prevention project under consideration completely eliminated the job or freed up sufficient time for the employee to perform some other task within the firm, there is no savings. This is often the case in small business in that the hazardous waste management duties are performed by the owner. Given that there is rarely any direct compensation for the number of hours worked for the small business owner, there is often no monetary human resource savings from the pollution prevention project.

In either case, computing the costs and/or benefits for human resources expense is straightforward. The number of hours required or saved by implementing the project are simply multiplied by the wages paid including hourly based benefits.

Training Expense

Pollution prevention investment may also involve the purchase of equipment or new, nonhazardous input materials which require additional operator training. In computing the total training costs, both the direct costs (e.g., tuition charges) and the worker-hours spent in training must be considered as an expense. In addition, any additional costs for refresher training or training for new employees over and above the current training requirements must be included in the analysis.

Computing the direct costs for training is simply a matter of adding the costs of tuition, travel, per diem, and so on for the involved employees. Similarly, to compute the human resource costs, the employee's wage rate is simply multiplied by the number of hours spent away from the job in training.

There has been discussion as to what hourly rate should be charged for the employees in such a situation. For any profitable firm, it is clear that an employee must earn more for the employer than the amount paid in hourly wages. Based on this line of thinking, it would be reasonable to charge the hourly training expense at the rate of an employee's earning power for the firm. However, traditionally the straight wage rate plus benefits such as pension and social security have been used in such calculations.

Floor Space Expense

As with opportunity costs, the floor space cost must be based on the value of alternative uses. For example, multiple rinse tanks have long been used to reduce the volume of rinse water in electroplating. If a single rinse tank of 50 square feet were replaced with a cascade rinse system of 65 square feet, then the floor space expense would be the financial worth of the extra 15 square feet and should be included as an expense in the financial analysis for the pollution prevention project.

Unfortunately, computing this floor space opportunity cost is not always as straightforward as computing training costs. For example, if the space needed for the cascade rinse system meant that a electroplating tank had to be removed, the floor space expense would be the revenue that the tank had generated. However, where little square footage is required, there may be no other use for the floor space, which implies a zero cost. Even if the area which will be lost by the equipment installation is currently only being used for storage of extra parts, bench stock, feed materials, and so on, the worth of having a drum of chemical or an extra part closer to the operator must be considered.

As square footage requirements increase, calculating floor space costs can become more straightforward. For example, if a new building was needed to house the pollution prevention equipment, it would be easy to compute a cost. Similarly, if installing the equipment at the production site displaces enough storage room to require that additional sheds be built, the cost would again be easy to compute.

As a default, the cost of floor space can be estimated from information available from realtors in the local area. The average square-foot cost for new or used warehouse, administrative, or production space that would be charged to procure the space on the local market is the average market worth of a square foot of floor space. Unless there is a specific alternative proposal for the floor space, this market analysis cost can be used as a proxy for calculations in the analysis.

Supply Expense

Items needed for the operation of the new equipment are included in the supply expense category if they are expendable. For example, consider the situation where an ion exchange system was being investigated as a method to remove metals from a process tank so that the solution could be reused instead of being discarded as hazardous waste. The ion exchange resins cannot be reused and must be replaced at regular intervals. These resins would be considered as supply expenses. They would be expended at their actual cost during their period of use and then reduced to present value during the analysis. Normal supplies such as office supplies generally are not included in the analysis as they are part of normal business overhead.

Depreciation Expense

Since nearly all procurement actions for pollution prevention investment involve the purchase of some equipment, how the equipment is expended is a critical consideration. To help clarify matters, there will be a distinction drawn between expense and cost. For example, if a company purchases a new vehicle for $15,000, it has incurred a cost equal to the purchase price for the vehicle. However, under the accrual accounting method which is most commonly used, companies report and/or record expenses and revenues during the accounting period in which they were incurred versus when the cash was either paid out or received. Hence, under accrual accounting, the $15,000 cash paid for the vehicle is a cost but not an expense. This becomes clear in looking at the accounting equation presented earlier:

$$\text{Assets} - \text{liabilities} = \text{owner's equity}$$

In purchasing the vehicle, the firm traded one asset (cash) for another asset (the vehicle). The owners equity was not changed, so no expense was involved in the transaction.

Many business expenditures are for supply items in that they are used up in the accounting period they are purchased. For example, pens, paper, gasoline, wages, rent, and so on are all items that are purchased and used on a weekly, monthly, or annual basis. Conversely, other assets remain usable for many accounting periods: buildings, machinery, vehicles, and so on. In this latter case, the method of expensing the cost for these items is called *depreciation*. Depreciation systematically allocates the cost of these assets as an expense of doing business over the periods in which they are used. Because there are specific, recognized, and accepted depreciation methods for allocating expenses, the actual market value of the asset may be quite different from the book value, i.e., the initial price less the amount expended.

The concept behind depreciation is that events occur which reduce an asset's value to the company, but if there is no loss in service value, such as would be the case with land, there is no depreciation. The factors that cause a decline in service value can be classified as either physical or function.

Physical factors are wear and tear, rust, weathering, and the like. Equipment just plain wears out. Conversely, *functional factors* mainly center around obsolescence. The easiest way to understand such functional factors is to think of the improvements made in the computer industry. Just a few years ago a "286" computer with both a floppy disk and a 4-meg hard drive was considered state of the art. Now, new machines with both speed and memories that are orders of magnitude higher are common and affordable. A company with the older 286 machines may have to replace them with newer computers which are capable of running current software to remain competitive, even though there has been no physical wear.

The automobile industry experiences a similar functional factor decline each year. Although the stamping dyes that are used to make body parts are still serviceable at the end of a model year, as each year's new model is introduced, the old model's manufacturing equipment becomes functionally obsolete.

In any event, prediction of the specific causes of depreciation is not essential for measuring the expenses to be computed against the use of an asset. In cases where the actual "life" of an asset is much longer or shorter than expected, the costs can be adjusted at the time the equipment is retired from service.

In historical cost accounting, the amount of cash (or cash equivalent) paid in acquiring an asset is the acquisition or historical cost. For example, if a new 486 computer were purchased for $2500, that would be the acquisition or historical cost. The asset's residual or salvage value is the amount expected to be received when the asset is retired from service; for example, the 486 computer may be sold upon retirement for some lesser value. As a result, the normal asset value which is depreciated is the acquisition or historical cost less the salvage value as that amount represents the portion of the asset used by the company.

This concept is akin to leasing versus purchasing an automobile. The idea is that leasing is cheaper because the lessee only pays for the portion of the auto's value which is actually used; purchase price less salvage value. In the case of leasing, the auto dealer estimates the worth of the vehicle at the end of the lease, subtracts that value from the purchase price, and charges the difference amortized over the lease period at a competitive interest rate. In this case, the automobile cost would be included in the analysis as an expense and not depreciated. Conversely, if the vehicle were purchased, the purchase price of the asset less its worth at retirement, the same dollar amount that the automobile dealer considered, would be the amount depreciated by the purchaser of the vehicle.

Estimating salvage value is necessarily a subjective skill, and, in the past, many arguments erupted between entrepreneurs and the Internal Revenue Service. As a result, the IRS code was amended to provide that salvage value may be ignored entirely in calculating depreciation for tax reporting. However, in preparation of financial statements and in cases such as selecting between investment alternatives, salvage value can be a major factor and should be included.

As was the case with salvage value, service life estimation is also subjective, and both physical and functional reductions of service life must be considered. In general, historical experience with similar assets is the best guide, but, especially in the case of obsolescence, many of the factors that determine the service life are outside the control of the company. As a result, initial service life estimates are often reexamined every few years with adjustments made to the initial estimates and the depreciation amounts.

In one case however, income tax reporting, no service life estimation is required. In 1981 and 1986 Congress enacted legislation, the Accelerated Cost Recovery System (ACRS—pronounced "akers"), which sets specific service lives. Under ACRS, nearly all assets are grouped into one of the following classes:

Service Life (years)	Asset Example
3	Some racehorses
5	Vehicles and some manufacturing and research and development equipment
7	Office equipment, railroad cars, and locomotives
10	Vessels, barges, and land improvements
20	Municipal sewers
27.5	Residential rental property
31.5	Nonresidential buildings

The service lives dictated by the tax code may be too long, too short, or approximately correct when compared to reality, but they must be used in income tax reporting. As a result, in the absence of other information such as historical records, they can serve as a guide in estimating the service life of pollution prevention equipment.

An additional consideration is the concept of repair and/or improvement of an asset. Repairs which are designed to maintain an asset at its present value are expenses and are written off completely during the accounting period in which they occur. Conversely, asset improvement increases the value of the asset and can often extend the service life. For example, if there is a power surge and a computer has a "head crash," one option would be to replace the affected drive with an identical unit. In this case, there could be a repair expense because the asset's service life was not changed. However, a second option would be if during the repair the computer were upgraded with expanded memory, new processors, and so on, the upgrade would represent an improvement to the asset. In this latter case, the value of the asset would change in proportion to the upgrade, the service life would probably be extended, the salvage value may change, and the depreciation cost per accounting period would change.

As mentioned earlier, there are a number of accepted depreciation methods. In addition to the ACRS (used in income tax calculation), the businesses today use four basic depreciation methods: straight-line time, straight-line production or use, declining balance, and sum-of-the-years digits.

Straight-line Time. Straight-line time is the most commonly used depreciation method for financial reporting and consists of reducing the value of an asset, the historical cost less salvage value, by a constant percentage of its worth each year. The computation is as follows:

$$\text{Annual depreciation (\$/year)} = \frac{\text{historical cost} - \text{salvage value}}{\text{estimated service life (years)}}$$

In some cases the cost to remove an asset from service exceeds its salvage value. This requires the excess removal cost to be treated as a negative salvage value and as a result, the cost of salvage is added to the historical cost. Negative salvage value could be involved in cases where hazardous waste cleanup is required. For example, when a plating shop in California was closed, the spills, vapors, and so on which permeated the concrete in the building meant that the entire building had to be disposed of in a hazardous waste landfill—a negative salvage value of over $960,000.

To illustrate straight-line time depreciation, assume a piece of pollution prevention equipment had a historical cost of $5000 and a salvage value of $500 and was expected to last 5 years. The annual depreciation expense calculation under straight-line time would be

$$\text{Annual depreciation expense} = \frac{\$5000 - \$500}{5 \text{ years}} = \$900/\text{year}$$

Straight-Line Production or Use. When assets are not used uniformly over the service life, as would be the case with seasonal equipment items such as snowplows, straight-line time depreciation may be inappropriate. In these cases, straight-line production or use depreciation may be the method of choice. Under this depreciation method, rather than estimating the service life, an estimate is made of the total use available in an asset such as the number of hours that a generator can be used or the number of "widgets" than can be manufactured by a piece of equipment. The depreciation expense calculation then becomes a two-step process in that first the cost per unit is computed:

$$\text{Depreciation per unit (\$/unit)} = \frac{\text{historical cost} - \text{salvage value}}{\text{estimated total number of units}}$$

The depreciation cost per accounting period is then computed by taking the number of units produced or used during the accounting period times the depreciation per unit.

To illustrate straight-line production or use depreciation, assume the pollution prevention equipment shown above was expected to last 10,000 hours and cost $5000, and had an estimated salvage value of $500. The most obvious depreciation method would be in cost per hour. The cost-per-unit calculation would be

$$\frac{\$5000 - \$500}{10,000 \text{ hours}} = \$0.45/\text{hour}$$

The depreciation expense per year would then be computed by multiplying the expense per hour ($0.45/hour) times the number of hours the machine was used in any given accounting period.

Note that if the machine were used on a regular basis, year around, the 40 hours per week, 50 weeks per year would result in 2000 hours × $0.45/hour or $900; the same depreciation expense that was calculated under the straight-line time method.

In many cases, the earning power of an asset decreases with the age of the asset—for example, tools may lose precision, rental properties may command less rent. In these cases the depreciation of an asset is accelerated with larger depreciation expenses taken in the early years of the service life and progressively smaller depreciation expenses taken in the latter years of the service life. The two most common accelerated depreciation methods are declining balance and sum-of-the-years'-digits.

Declining Balance.   Unlike the previous two depreciation methods, the declining balance method does not base each year's depreciation expense on the historical cost less the salvage value. Instead, there are two significant differences. First, the value of the asset is recomputed after each accounting period, and the depreciation is based on the new book value. Second, the initial value is taken as the historical cost, and the salvage value is not subtracted. Depreciation expense is then computed for each accounting period by a set percentage under the constraint that the asset's book value cannot be reduced below its salvage value. Further, to allow for the maximum depreciation expense, when the depreciation amount calculated under the declining balance method becomes less than what would result from applying straight-line time depreciation over the remaining life of the asset, the straight-line time depreciation value is used.

The amount of depreciation expended in any given year is a percentage of the asset's value based on the years of service life. This percentage is calculated by expressing the service life as a reciprocal (e.g., a 10-year service life would be expressed as 1/10th or 0.1) multiplied by a factor. The factors most commonly used are 200 percent (i.e., double declining balance) or 150 percent. Hence, in double declining balance, the amount of depreciation taken each year would be (200 percent) × 0.1 or 20 percent per year subject to the constraints listed above.

To illustrate declining balance, the pollution prevention equipment previously used will again be considered, equipment purchased for $5000 with a salvage value of $500 and a service life of 5 years. The percentage or rate of depreciation, using the double declining balance, would be 1/5 years × 200 percent = 40 percent/year, and the depreciation expense would be as follows:

Year	Depreciation rate	Accumulated depreciation	Book value	Annual depreciation
1	0.40	0	$5000	$2000
2	0.40	$2000	3000	1200
3	0.40	3200	1800	720
4	N/A	3920	1080	540*
5	N/A	4460	540	40†

*During year 4, the straight-line method is used because it results in a higher depreciation cost, i.e., $1080 book value/2 years remaining service life > $1080 × (0.4).

†The depreciation in year 5 was reduced to $40 because the book value of the asset could not be reduced below the salvage value.

Sum-of-the-Years' Digits. The sum-of-the-years'-digits is the other commonly used accelerated depreciation method and represents something of a highbred of the other methods. Like the straight-line methods, the sum-of-the-years'-digits method requires that salvage value be included in the initial value of the asset, and the depreciation expense is calculated from this initial value each year. Conversely, like declining balance, the depreciation expense is highest in the first year and is reduced during each additional year over the service life.

The percentage of the value which is depreciated during each accounting period is calculated by multiplying the historical cost less salvage value by an increasingly smaller fraction each year over the life of the asset. The numerator in the reduction fraction used each year to calculate the annual depreciation is simply the number of years of service life remaining at the *beginning* of the accounting period. The denominator is the sum of all the years of service life—hence the name sum-of-the-years'-digits.

Again using the same piece of pollution prevention equipment (a $5000 cost, a 5-year service life, and a $500 salvage value) to illustrate the sum-of-the-years'-digits method, the denominator of the reduction fraction would be $1 + 2 + 3 + 4 + 5 = 15$. Hence, the depreciation fraction at a time when there were 3 years of service life left in the asset would be $3/15 = 20$ percent. The depreciation schedule over the 5-year equipment life, under the sum-of-the-years'-digits method, would be

Years left	Depreciation fraction	Annual depreciation	Accumulated depreciation
5	5/15	$1500	$1500
4	4/15	1200	2700
3	3/15	900	3600
2	2/15	600	4200
1	1/15	300	4500

Note that the total accumulated depreciation under the sum-of-the-years'-digits must be equal to the historical cost less salvage value.

Accelerated Cost Recovery System. As previously stated, the accelerated cost recovery system (ACRS) depreciation method is used for income tax reporting and is subject to changes in the Internal Revenue Code. As a result, it shall not be discussed as an optional method to develop depreciation costs in pollution prevention investment comparison. However, it was designed to allow some flexibility on the part of the equipment owner. For items whose useful lives are typically shorter than the required service lives, the method allows for either 150 percent or 200 percent declining balance methods to be used. Further, salvage value is ignored in the calculation of ACRS depreciation, so when an asset whose entire value was depreciated is sold, the profit resulting from the sale must be considered a capital gain.

The most relevant question becomes which depreciation method is best to use in pollution prevention investment analysis. Recalling the profit equation, the key to maximizing the projected profit resulting from investment in pollution prevention normally lies in minimizing expense factor in the equation. If the selection criteria of net present value is used, the net present value should be maximized. Hence, the present value of pure expense elements connected with the pollution prevention option should be minimized.

To show the effect of the various depreciation methods on the profit equation, the following is a summary of the present value of the annual depreciation expenses for the $5000 pollution prevention equipment under each of the methods discussed:

Year	Straight-line		Double declining balance	Sum-of-years' digits
	Time	Use		
1	$900	$900	$2000	$1500
2	900	900	1200	1200
3	900	900	720	900
4	900	900	540	600
5	900	900	40	300
PV	$3412	$3412	$3745	$3628

In general, as shown above, to minimize the expense of the investment, thereby maximizing the net present value, straight-line time should be used because it reflects the smallest present value of expenses.

Two other factors could affect the investment decision and bear consideration: cash flow and opportunity cost. The first, *cash flow*, does not have a direct effect on the firm's revenues or expenses; however, the concept must be considered in analyzing any investment opportunity, pollution prevention projects notwithstanding. There are three aspects to a cash purchase which can affect a firm's available cash. First, cash must be used at the time of purchase. Second, it takes time to realize financial returns from the project through enhanced revenues or decreased expenses. Finally, depreciation expense is calculated much more slowly than the rate at which the cash was spent. This implies that as a result of making an economically sound investment, a firm could find itself cash poor, a situation which must be considered before making the investment.

Conversely, pollution prevention efforts can have a very positive effect on cash flow. For example, if a pollution prevention investment eliminated a hazardous waste via an input material substitution it could result in a large amount of cash available to the firm from not having to pay for hazardous waste disposal every 90 days. Hence, even though cash flow does not have a direct impact on revenues and expenses, the concept must be considered in analyzing pollution prevention projects.

The second factor, *opportunity cost,* is not as straightforward. If in purchasing pollution prevention equipment a firm pays for the project out of its own cash reserves, some feel this action should be reflected in the analysis because the cash cannot otherwise be invested—a cost assigned to the action which represents the lost opportunity. The basis of the argument is that if cash is used on pollution prevention, it is unavailable to use for other opportunities or investments. As a result, revenues which could have been generated by the cash (e.g., interest from a certificate of deposit at a bank) should be treated as an expense to reduce the value of the pollution prevention project.

Although the reasoning seems sound, opportunity costs are not expenses. It is true that the cash will be unavailable for other investments; however, opportunity cost should be thought of as a comparison criteria and not an expense. The opportunity forgone by using the cash is considered when the pollution prevention project competes for the firm's funds. In general, it is expressed as the hurdle rate or the minimum percent return on capital depending upon the financial analysis criteria discussed earlier (e.g., net value of present worth, internal rate of return). It is this competition for the firm's funds that encompasses opportunity cost, so it should not be accounted directly against the project's benefits unless the firm bases its financial decisions on economic versus accounting profit. If return on investment is considered as an expense, as would be the case in economic profit, then such checks on the suitability of the investment such as the hurdle rate or minimum return on capital invested should not be used.

For example, a minimum rate of return or hurdle rate is often used to express this opportunity cost competition between investments. If a firm can draw 10 percent interest on cash in the bank, then 10 percent would be a valid choice for the hurdle rate as it represents the firm's cash opportunity cost. Therefore, in analyzing investment options under this return on investment criteria, not only would the highest returns be selected, but any project which pays the firm a return less than the 10 percent hurdle rate would not be considered. If the opportunity cost of the project were also included in the analysis as an expense, then a project which showed a 2 percent internal rate of return (with the opportunity cost included) would not be accepted when in actuality the 2 percent internal rate of return would be over and above the 10 percent hurdle rate because the opportunity cost had already been included as an expense.

Case Study: Financial Analysis of a Solvent Process

To outline the principles discussed above, this case study provides a step-by-step analysis of a pollution prevention investment; the reader should be able to recognize each of the seven steps in the financial analysis. While the standard accounting formats such as T accounts will not be used, the expenses will be analyzed using the accounting classifications presented earlier in this section.

The hypothetical firm under review takes in used parts, cleans them in dip tanks using a chlorinated solvent, and applies a new finish. To simplify the analysis, it is assumed that the first step, determining investment alternatives, has been accomplished and the investment alternatives under consideration are all technically acceptable. Hence, the financial analysis will be between three investment opportunities: the current solvent cleaning operation and two pollution prevention alternatives—a solvent recycling system and nonhazardous material substitution.

Baseline

As indicated before, the first step is to define the baseline cost of the process. Once this is accomplished, the financial effects of any change to business as usual can be judged as either equal to, more expensive (an expense), than or cheaper (a revenue) than the baseline case. Figure 3-2 shows the material balance for the

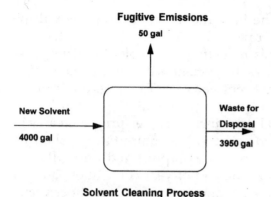

Solvent Cleaning Process

Figure 3-2. Baseline material balance.

current system. With the mass balance complete, baseline annual costs can be computed for the process. As before, although these costs are being computed on a per-tank basis, they could be multiplied by the total number of tanks. Assuming only one tank, the resulting baseline costs would be as shown in Table 3-3.

None of the other expenses previously discussed in Sec. 2 need to be addressed at this point, since they will be computed, as applicable, as changes from business-as-usual costs.

To express these annual costs in present value terms, a time reference must be selected so that each option can be considered over the same length of time. Since the recycle equipment being considered has an expected life of 10 years and both the business-as-usual and material substitution processes can continue

Table 3-3. Baseline Cost Analysis

Element	Rate	Annual cost
Procurement expense	n/a	0
Operating expense:		
Utilities	n/c	n/c
Operating expense	n/c	n/c
Input solvent	$3.50/gallon	$14,000
Waste disposal	$2.50/gallon	$9,875

over any time period, the baseline and both options will be examined over this 10-year period.

To make the example as realistic as possible, the firm's discount rate shall be taken as 10 percent with an assumed inflation rate at a constant 5 percent per year. To reflect the increase in prices from inflation, all future costs will be inflated by the inflation rate plus any real price increases (i.e., price increases in excess of inflation). All present value computations shall be made using 10 percent interest, compounded annually, all expenses/revenues will use the end-of-year convention, and all expenses shall be increased at a minimum of 5 percent per year.

To account for prices which rise faster than inflation, annual real price increases (in excess of inflation) of 1 percent of the annual solvent cost and 4 percent of the annual disposal cost shall be assumed. In these cases, the cost of solvent shall increase 6 percent per year (5 percent inflation + 1 percent real price increase), and, similarly, waste disposal shall increase 9 percent per year. Given these assumptions, the baseline expenses for the next decade are as shown in Table 3-4. As shown earlier, these costs can also be shown on a time line with arrows or bars down reflecting expenses and up reflecting revenues as done in Fig. 3-3.

In many cases firms simplify the calculations by assuming costs will be constant over the life of the project. If this is the case, then the method to compute the out-year costs would be identical to the method used in the example shown in Table 3-2.

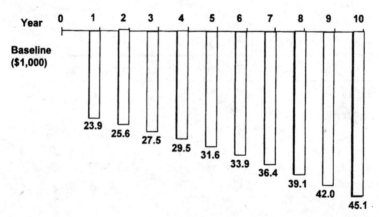

Figure 3-3. Time line of 10-year baseline costs.

Table 3-4. Ten-Year Baseline Costs

Year	Item	Annual costs without recycling	Annual total
1	New solvent	$14,000	
	Waste disposal	9,875	$23,875
2	New solvent	14,840	
	Waste disposal	10,764	25,604
3	New solvent	15,730	
	Waste disposal	11,732	27,463
4	New solvent	16,674	
	Waste disposal	12,788	29,463
5	New solvent	17,675	
	Waste disposal	13,939	31,614
6	New solvent	18,735	
	Waste disposal	15,194	33,929
7	New solvent	19,859	
	Waste disposal	16,561	36,421
8	New solvent	21,051	
	Waste disposal	18,052	39,103
9	New solvent	22,314	
	Waste disposal	19,677	41,990
10	New solvent	23,653	
	Waste disposal	21,447	45,100
Total annual costs			$334,561

The final step in establishing the baseline is to express these expenses as a single, present value sum to serve as the basis for comparing the pollution prevention options. This will be done for the baseline and both options simultaneously at the end of the analysis. At that time, with all annual costs computed, either the net cost, in cases where the option's annual costs are more expensive than the baseline, or net benefit, in cases where the option's annual costs are less expensive than the baseline, for each option will be brought back with present value calculations. Further, this allows the simplification to be made using offsetting costs.

Examining Pollution Prevention
Option 1—Recycle

As before, the first step is to establish the mass balance diagram for this option. This is shown in Fig. 3-4. As is the case with many recycle options, a salable by-product is generated (the recycled solvent), but instead of offering the solvent for sale, the firm is using it as an input to offset the cost of new solvent, so there is no revenue impact. Further, since the actual mechanics and materials for the cleaning operation have not changed, there should be no change in production rate as a result of this option. Thus there are no revenue impacts to consider, and, given that the same equipment will be used with the recycle option, the impacts on the other expense categories are minimized.

This material balance in Fig. 3-4 can be readily converted to a cash flow. As discussed earlier, the recovery equipment has a life of 10 years. Further, there is no salvage value, and no additional environmental permits, such as RCRA treatment permits or air permits, are required to operate or install the equipment. However, to avoid oversimplifying the example, we will assume

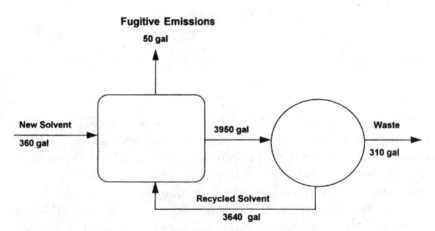

Figure 3-4. Material balance for the recycle system.

that the solvent must be chemically treated in year 5, at a cost of $1000, to retain it's effectiveness; this will be treated in the same manner as a supply expense fully expended during the accounting period it occurs. Given these assumptions, the costs for the recycle system are as shown in Table 3-5.

Other expenses to consider include:

Insurance. The recycle operation involves a heated drum evaporator which could increase insurance expense. However, for simplicity, constant insurance expenses shall be assumed.

Depreciation. As discussed earlier, the straight-line time method of depreciation shall be used with the procurement costs (historical value less salvage value) being expended at 10 percent each year for 10 years.

Interest. It will be assumed the firm had to borrow the capital costs and will make equal, annual payments for 3 years at the end of each year. The interest expense will be based on 12 percent of the loan balance at the beginning of each year.

Table 3-5. Costs for Solvent Recycling

Element	Rate	Annual expense	
Procurement expenses:			
Recycling equipment		$40,500	
Tanks, pumps, mixers, etc.		7,000	
Design		5,000	
Piping, labor, etc.		8,000	
Contingency (at 10 percent)		6,000	
			$66,500
Operation expenses:			
Utilities		$240	
Labor	1 hour/day at $20/hour	5,000	
Maintenance/spares (at 5 percent of cap cost)		3,325	
			$8,565
Input solvent	$3.50/gallon	1,260	
Waste disposal	$2.50/gallon	775	

Human resources.   The equipment requires 1 hour of maintenance per day. This expense (at $20/hour based on 50 weeks' operation per year) has been included in the operations expenses listed in Table 3-5. For simplicity, the wage rate will be assumed constant except for cost-of-living increases equal to the rate of inflation.

Training.   The direct training costs were included by the recycle equipment supplier as part of the procurement price. We are assuming that the training will take place on site, so there will be no direct costs for travel, tuition, and so on. However, three operators must spend 2 hours each learning the operations. Their wage cost will also be taken as $20/hour.

Floor space considerations.   The equipment is relatively compact, will be installed integral to the process, and will carry a zero floor space expense.

Utilities.   The added utility costs have been included in the above table and will be increased each year by the inflation rate as part of the category operating expenses.

Supplies.   The $1000 expense for treating the solvent in year 5 will be included in the out-year expenses. Given that this expense was agreed to as part of the sales contract for the equipment, it will not be inflated.

As done with the baseline, annual costs for the recycling option must also be spread over time as they will actually occur. Given the interest, inflation, and similar assumptions, the costs, by year, for the 10-year life are shown in Table 3-6.

As before, these costs can be shown on a time line as shown in Fig. 3-5. These annual costs will be compared to the baseline after all cash flows for the options have been computed.

Examining Pollution Prevention
Option 2—Material Substitution

Especially in pollution prevention projects which involve substituting a nonhazardous material for a hazardous material, part of the step 1 analysis must consider how well the new product or process performs in relation to the current practice. In this

Table 3-6. Ten-Year Costs for Recycle Option

Year	Item	Costs with recycle	Total
1	Interest expense	$7,980	
	Depreciation expense	6,650	
	Initial training	120	
	Operating expenses	8,565	
	New solvent	1,260	
	Waste disposal	775	
			$25,350
2	Interest expense	$5,320	
	Depreciation expense	6,650	
	Operating expenses	8,993	
	New solvent	1,336	
	Waste disposal	845	
			$23,144
3	Interest expense	$2,660	
	Depreciation expense	6,650	
	Operating expenses	9,443	
	New solvent	1,416	
	Waste disposal	921	
			$21,089
4	Depreciation expense	$6,650	
	Operating expenses	9,915	
	New solvent	1,501	
	Waste disposal	1,004	
			$19,069
5	Depreciation expense	$6,650	
	Operating expenses	11,411	
	New solvent	1,591	
	Waste disposal	1,094	
			$20,746
6	Depreciation expense	$6,650	
	Operating expenses	10,932	
	New solvent	1,686	
	Waste disposal	1,192	
			$20,460

Table 3-6. Ten-Year Costs for Recycle Option
(*Continued*)

Year	Item	Costs with recycle	Total
7	Depreciation expense	$6,650	
	Operating expenses	11,478	
	New solvent	1,787	
	Waste disposal	1,300	
			$21,215
8	Depreciation expense	$6,650	
	Operating expenses	12,052	
	New solvent	1,895	
	Waste disposal	1,417	
			$22,013
9	Depreciation expense	$6,650	
	Operating expenses	12,655	
	New solvent	2,008	
	Waste disposal	1,544	
			$22,857
10	Depreciation expense	$6,650	
	Operating expenses	13,287	
	New solvent	2,129	
	Waste disposal	1,683	
			$23,749
Total annual costs			$219,693

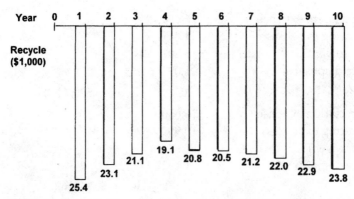

Figure 3-5. Time line for 10-year recycle option costs.

example, it is assumed no operational changes are required so production levels can be maintained. However, the cost of the nonhazardous solvent is nearly 25 percent higher: $4.60/gallon. With the same assumptions regarding solvent and wastewater treatment cost increases, the first-year costs for switching to the nonhazardous solvent would be as shown in Table 3-7.

Other expenses to consider include

Insurance. Since the material substitution operation involves less risk to the employees, there could be an insurance reduction; however, because insurance cost is very site- and circumstance-specific, and to not bias the analysis, it will again be assumed to be constant.

Depreciation. Since there is no capital expenditure, there is no equipment to depreciate.

Interest. The company has the cash reserve to absorb the additional solvent cost without borrowing any additional capital. Hence, there is no interest expense.

Human resources. There is no additional equipment maintenance requirement, and the wage rate is again treated as a constant except for cost-of-living increases due to inflation.

Training. As before, it will be assumed the training needed to use the new solvent was supplied by the vendor, and three operators spent 2 hours each learning how to handle, test, and

Table 3-7. First-Year Costs for Material Substitution

Element	Rate	One-time costs
Procurement expenses:		n/a
Training		$120
		Annual expenses
Operating expenses:		
Operating costs		n/c
Maintenance/spare parts		n/c
Input solvent	$4.60/gallon	$18,400
Waste disposal		$0

maintain the solvent. Their wage rate will be taken as $20/hour as in the recycle option.

Floor space considerations.   The current solvent storage capacity for the firm is adequate for the new solvent.

Supplies.   The only supply costs involved are those related to purchasing solvent each year.

The annual solvent substitution costs, increased at the appropriate rate, are shown over the 10-year lifetime in Table 3-8.

The time line would be as shown in Fig. 3-6.

Making the Final Decision

With all annual costs computed, the final ranking of the investment alternatives can be done. One option would be to show the investment options pair-wise on a single time line. For example, Figs. 3-7 and 3-8 show the time lines for the recycle and material substitution options respectively. In each case, the business-as-usual option is shown as a benefit or revenue in that if the individual option were chosen, the business-as-usual costs would be avoided.

Table 3-8. Ten-Year Material Substitution Costs

Year	Item	Annual cost
1	New solvent and training	$18,520
2	New solvent	19,504
3	New solvent	20,674
4	New solvent	21,915
5	New solvent	23,230
6	New solvent	24,623
7	New solvent	26,101
8	New solvent	27,667
9	New solvent	29,327
10	New solvent	31,086

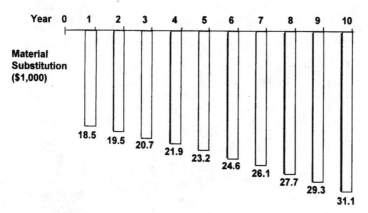

Figure 3-6. Time line for 10-year material substitution costs.

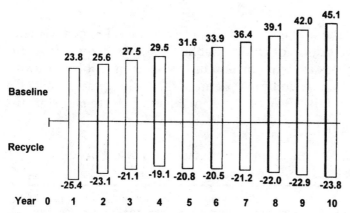

Figure 3-7. Time line comparison of business-as-usual versus the recycle option.

   This method shows the simplification discussed earlier. One method which could be used to compare the three options would be to compute the net present value of each option separately. Conversely, the net revenue or expense for each year can be computed and that delta brought back to present time. If the delta is positive, the option is financially advantageous, and the positive net present value reflects the savings available to the firm if the option were selected. In this case, since there are three options, the delta computation must be repeated twice; the

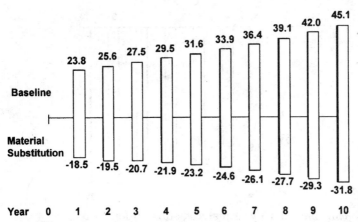

Figure 3-8. Time line comparison of business-as-usual versus the material substitution option.

option with the highest, positive net present value of the deltas would be the option of choice. Table 3-9 shows the year and the annual business as usual or baseline costs from Table 3-4 in the first two columns; columns 3 and 4 show the annual costs for recycle from Table 3-6 and the increase or decrease from the

Table 3-9. Annual Cost Comparison for the Three Investment Options

Year	Annual BAU	Annual recycle	Delta	Annual sol sub	Delta
1	$23,875	$25,350	($1,475)	$18,520	$5,355
2	25,604	23,144	2,460	19,504	6,100
3	27,463	21,089	6,374	20,674	6,789
4	29,463	19,069	10,394	21,915	7,548
5	31,614	20,746	10,868	23,230	8,384
6	33,929	20,460	13,469	24,623	9,306
7	36,421	21,215	15,206	26,101	10,320
8	39,103	22,013	17,090	27,667	11,436
9	41,990	22,857	19,133	29,327	12,663
10	45,100	23,749	21,351	31,086	14,014
Totals			$114,870		$91,915

baseline respectively; and finally, columns 5 and 6 show the annual costs for material substitution from Table 3-8 and their associated change from the baseline.

The time line makes working with deltas particularly simple. Figures 3-9 and 3-10 show the net revenue or expense during each accounting period for the recycle and material substitution options respectively.

Although it is generally simpler for work with deltas, either the deltas or the annual costs can be brought back to present value. To demonstrate how each is done and to verify that the results are equivalent, both methods shall be shown. Table 3-10 shows the

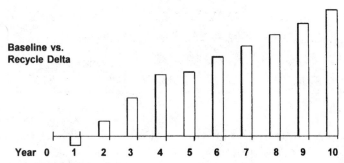

Figure 3-9. Time line comparison of the business-as-usual versus recycle option deltas.

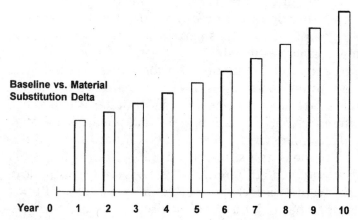

Figure 3-10. Time line comparison of the business-as-usual versus material substitution option deltas.

Table 3-10. Present Value Computations for the Three Options (at 10 Percent Interest Compounded Annually)

Year	Annual BAU	PV BAU	Annual recycle	PV recycle	Annual sol sub	PV sol sub
1	$23,875	$21,705	$25,350	$23,045	$18,520	$16,836
2	25,604	21,160	23,144	19,127	19,504	16,119
3	27,463	20,633	21,089	15,844	20,674	15,533
4	29,463	20,124	19,069	13,024	21,915	14,968
5	31,614	19,630	20,746	12,882	23,230	14,424
6	33,929	19,152	20,460	11,549	24,623	13,899
7	36,421	18,690	21,215	10,887	26,101	13,394
8	39,103	18,242	22,013	10,269	27,667	12,907
9	41,990	17,808	22,857	9,694	29,327	12,438
10	45,100	17,388	23,749	9,156	31,086	11,985
Total PVs		$194,531		$135,478		$142,503

results of the calculations when the total annual costs for each accounting period are computed at their net present value.

In this example, the present value totals in the table, $195,000, $136,000 and $143,000, can be taken as the total sum of monies the firm would have to set aside today, at a 10 percent interest rate, to pay for the three options over the next 10 years. Under the investment criterion of net present value, it is apparent that both the recycle option and the substitution option are superior to continuing business as usual.

The net present value calculations for the deltas or differences between the annual costs can likewise be computed and are shown in Table 3-11. Because this analysis of deltas is concerned with the differences between the options and business as usual, there are only two answers because the comparative value is zero for the business-as-usual option, i.e., if no changes are made, there would be no difference in cost. As shown in Table 3-11, if the firm were to select the recycle or solvent substitution investment options, it would enjoy pretax profit increases (expressed as decreased expenses) of $59,000 and $52,000 respectively for the two options. As one would expect, if the

Table 3-11. Annual Cost Comparison for the Three Investment Options (at 10 Percent Annual Interest Based on the Annual Differences)

Year	Annual BAU	Annual recycle	Delta	Recycle delta PV	Annual sol sub	Delta	Sol sub delta PV
1	$23,875	$25,350	($1,475)	($1,341)	$18,520	$5,355	$4,868
2	25,604	23,144	2,460	2,033	19,504	6,100	5,041
3	27,463	21,089	6,374	4,789	20,674	6,789	5,101
4	29,463	19,069	10,394	7,099	21,915	7,548	5,155
5	31,614	20,746	10,868	6,748	23,230	8,384	5,206
6	33,929	20,460	13,469	7,603	24,623	9,306	5,253
7	36,421	21,215	15,206	7,803	26,101	10,320	5,296
8	39,103	22,013	17,090	7,973	27,667	11,436	5,335
9	41,990	22,857	19,133	8,114	29,327	12,663	5,370
10	45,100	23,749	21,351	8,232	31,086	14,014	5,403
Totals				$59,053			$52,028

present value of the deltas is added to the present value of either option, the result will be the present value of the business as usual calculation. Again, the firm would be wise to select one of the two pollution prevention options.

Given that the business-as-usual option is clearly less desirable, the final task is to select between the two pollution prevention options. Although the initial reaction would be to invest in the recycle equipment, two intangible factors must be considered. First, there is uncertainty in the analysis: Will the recycle equipment actually last 10 years? Will the solvent prices change faster or slower than predicted? In this case, the difference in the two options is only a savings of $7000—approximately 12 percent. Depending upon the analyst, if both calculations are only expected to be ± 10 percent accurate, the two figures, $59,000 and $52,000, are essentially equivalent.

This "equivalency" brings up the second point. As previously discussed, when projects appear financially equivalent or nearly so given the potential uncertainties, consideration of other tier 1, 2, and 3 costs can swing favor toward one option or the other.

If one were to consider the labor savings due to not having to manifest waste shipments, label drums, and so on, because the material substitution option eliminates hazardous waste generation, there could be a substantial savings. In addition, the elimination of hazardous waste limits the potential intangible tier 2 and 3 costs for remedial actions, lawsuits, and so on as well as giving a potential revenue boost in that the company can be seen as making improvements to benefit the environment. Given these considerations, material substitution may be the more beneficial option.

Conclusions

The key point to remember is firms are in business to make profit and, via reduced expenses, pollution prevention can be a critical element. Contrary to past views, environmental departments are not pure cost sinks with no payback potential. In the arena of pollution prevention, there are a number of areas where expenditures can be cut and profits increased by significant amounts.

There is no doubt that environmental management or mismanagement can impact a company's bottom line. The task for the environmental manager becomes one of selling the expense side of the profit equation. Reducing an expense is as effective as increasing revenues when it comes to generating profit. Even in cases where an investment in pollution prevention cannot be shown to reduce expenses, there can be a drastic effect on cash flow.

The final consideration in justifying pollution prevention investments are the tier 2 and 3 considerations. Any project proposed can affect revenues, expenses, and/or cash flow, but one would be hard pressed to name any other projects with the intangible effects carried by pollution prevention efforts. Although difficult to express in concrete financial terms, both increased environmental compliance and reduced pollution from such projects can have far ranging benefits in terms of reduced long-term liability, customer relations, public goodwill, and so on. Although these factors may not serve to justify the investment in a project by themselves, they must enter into the analysis.

Appendix 3A   The Effects of Income Tax

Although many firms use only revenue and expense figures in comparing investment projects, income tax effects can enter into any calculation which changes either revenues or expenses from the baseline values; more expenses mean lower profits but less taxes and vice versa. If the effect of the investment on net profit (i.e., after-tax profit) must be computed, the computations are simple and can be done during or after the analysis.

As with expenses and revenues, the total tax liability for each option does not need to be computed. Instead, only the difference in tax liability resulting from the changes in revenues and/or expenses from the baseline due to the options being considered is required.

The profit equation previously shown reflects gross or pretax profits. Income tax is based on the gross profit figure from this equation and cannot be computed until the changes in revenues and/or expenses are known. The net profit (NP) equation follows, for the purpose of illustration, with the income tax rate taken as constant at 40 percent of gross profit (GP):

$$NP = GP - (GP \times 0.40)$$

As the net profit equation shows, income taxes act to reduce the impact on net profit due to changes in gross profit brought about by different revenues and/or expenses: If revenues increase $100 with no other changes, gross or pretax profits would also increase $100. Since income taxes take $40 of this increase, the effect on net profit would be to reduce the effect of the $100 revenue increase to a $60 net profit increase. Similarly, if expenses increase $100, gross profit would decrease $100 and, as above, the tax liability would be $40 less. Hence, in this latter case, the $-$100 pre-profit impact would be mitigated to a $60 net profit decrease.

This implies that the profit impact of an increase or decrease in revenues or expenses is limited by 1 minus the tax rate $(1 - t)$. If the tax rate is different from 40 percent, it can be inserted into the $(1 - t)$ expression and used in calculating the impact. For example, for a 33 percent tax rate, a $100 increase in revenue would increase profit by $(1 - 0.33)$ or $67.

Tax credits are a special write-off that is allowed by the IRS at various times. For example, during the energy crisis in the 1970s, certain capital expenses that reduced energy consumption (such as solar energy projects) were given special treatment as tax credits. Unlike the more familiar personal tax deductions that only act to reduce taxable income, tax credits are deducted directly from the tax obligation of a firm. As a result, in this special tax credit case, capital expenses which would otherwise lower pretax income can be subtracted directly from the tax liability and increase profit. Although currently no projects are eligible for such tax credits, given the political emphasis on pollution prevention, it is a possibility for the future that cannot be overlooked.

Appendix 3B   Present Value Computation under Uncertainty

Tier 2 and 3 costs are by their nature very difficult to quantify or predict. For example, a typical tier 3 cost would be cost of lost sales or the devaluation of common stock value due to adverse public reaction to a pollution incident. The variables that would have to be considered in such a financial calculation would include the types of incidents that could occur, the severity of each incident, the ability of the firm to control or respond to the emergency, the public's reaction to the incident, the firm's ability to sate the public's concerns, and so on. As shown in various environmental incidents such as the Alaskan oil spill by the Exxon Valdez, predicting the impact of such incidents is complex at the very least.

Conversely, in many cases, there is a probability that can be connected with an event which can enter directly into the present value computation through the calculation of expected value. The expected value of an event is the probability of an event occurring times the cost or benefit of the event:

$$EV = (\$_{ben}) \times (prob_{ben}) - (\$_{cost}) \times (prob_{cost})$$

Once all expected values are determined, they are totaled and brought back to present value as done with any other benefit or expense. It is critical to remember that expected value is based on probability, and, as such, it serves as a measure of the central tendency or the value that an outcome would have on the average. In considering any single event, expected value is only predictive and should not be taken as an absolute value in much the same way that it is not unheard of to have two 100-year rainfall events occur within a few years of each other.

Gambling is based on expected value estimates. Although any individual can be on a "hot streak," the central tendency or average outcome can be predicted through expected value. For example, consider the simple game of roulette where one places a bet on any single number with the potential payoff of 36 to 1; however, there are 38 possible numbers if one considers "0" and "00." Hence, the expected value (EV) of a $1.00 bet can be calculated as follows:

$$EV = (\$36.00) \times (1/38) - (\$1.00) \times (37/38) = (\$0.947) - (0.974) = -\$0.027$$

The expected value analysis shows that on the average, the house will make, or the player will lose, $0.027. Whereas a 2.7 cent profit margin may not seem like much, it favors the house, and, given enough players, many casinos thrive on such margins.

In much the same manner that casinos predict revenues and expenses, probability can be used to investigate tier 2 and 3 expenses. For example, there is a great deal of data available from Occupational Safety and Health Administration (OSHA) studies regarding employee injury in the workplace. In justifying a material substitution pollution prevention project, if the probability of injury and a cost (such as the average number of days of work missed) could be found in literature or from historical records at the company or trade association, the benefit of a project could be computed. The expected value would be the monetary cost of not sustaining an injury multiplied by the probability of not sustaining an injury and subtracting the cost of incurring an injury times the probability of incurring an injury. Although this may sound complex, in general, there is no cost associated with not sustaining an injury, so only the second term, the probability of injury times the cost of the injury, need be considered.

In citing the recycle option examined above, it can be assumed that there is an injury potential due to the heated solvent still. If it can be assumed that the cost of an injury was 3 days of missed work, and the annual probability of the injury was .14, the benefit of eliminating that hazard would be (8 hours/day) × (3 days) × ($20/hour) × (.14) = $67. This may seem like a very small benefit, but other factors such as the number of employees, repeated probability for each year, additional costs due to hospitalization, treatment, and so on may also affect the calculation.

The concept of expected value is not complicated, although the calculations can become somewhat involved. For example, even though each individual's chance of injury may be small, given the number of employees, their individual opportunity costs, the various probabilities for each task, and so on, it could require a number of separate calculations. However, if one considers the effect of the sum of these small costs, or the large potential costs of environmental lawsuits or site remediation under either the Resource Conservation and Recovery Act (RCRA) or the Comprehensive Environmental Response, Compensation, and Liability Act (CERCLA), the expected value computations can be quite important in the financial analysis. Included in the appendix to the next chapter is an example which shows how such an uncertainty analysis can be performed on estimating the long-term cleanup liability for depositing hazardous waste in a landfill.

Study Concepts

1. Be able to define *expected value*.
2. Given probabilities (expected values), be able to compute expected value (probability).
3. Be able to explain the difference between a balance sheet and an income statement.

4. Be able to support or deny the contention that a profitable company can go bankrupt because it is "cash poor."

5. Be able to discuss the difference between accounting and economic profit.

6. Be able to discuss McHugh's four tiers of potential project costs.

7. Given capital, operating, and other expenses and benefits, be able to compute the present worth of a pollution prevention project.

8. Be able to discuss opportunity cost and develop and support a position on how it should be considered in a financial analysis.

9. Be able to define *depreciation*.

10. Be able to compute depreciation under (*a*) straight-line, (*b*) declining balance, and (*c*) sum-of-the-years'-digits methods.

11. Be able to explain what the ACRS is and what it is used for.

4

The Mechanics of Establishing Pollution Prevention Alternatives

Preventing pollution is not a new concept. A number of companies established hazardous waste reduction programs in response to the requirements of the Resource Conservation and Recovery Act of 1986. In writing the implementing regulations for the legislation, the regulators state, "it shall be a condition of any permit issued . . . for the treatment, storage or disposal of hazardous waste . . . that the permittee certify . . . that the generator of the hazardous waste has a program in place to reduce the volume or quantity and toxicity of such waste to the degree determined by the generator to be economically practicable." In this same vein, the Comprehensive Environmental Response, Compensation and Liability Act (CERCLA) set the requirements for hazardous waste generators to evaluate and document their procedures for controlling the environmental impact of their operations.

These two acts, along with a realization that reducing waste increased a company's bottom line, led to major efforts throughout the country in hazardous waste reduction. However, Congress and the Environmental Protection Agency wanted the generators to go farther. There were a number of laudable hazardous waste reduction efforts, such as a dewatering system installed by the Air Force which increased the percentage of solids in the sludge from an industrial waste treatment plant from a few percent to 70 to 80 percent, but there was a feeling that there had to be a better way to approach pollution prevention.

The basic question was whether this type of minimization effort was actually waste reduction. For example, in the typical case of dewatering sludge, there is no question that the action reduces the volume of the waste sent for disposal; however, the actual mass of the waste was unchanged. In fact, in many of the reduction efforts, only the concentration of waste was affected and not a reduction of the mass of waste remaining. As a result, in 1990, Congress passed the Pollution Prevention Act.

Pollution Prevention Act of 1990

One of the critical consequences of the passage of the Pollution Prevention Act was to define more precisely *pollution prevention* as opposed to *hazardous waste minimization*. Congress had the clear intent of shifting emphasis away from treatment options toward actually avoiding waste generation. To emphasize this point, Congress defined the pollution prevention hierarchy in Section 2 of the Pollution Prevention Act as follows:

> Findings and Policy: This section establishes a Pollution Prevention hierarchy as a national policy, declaring that:
>
> ▪ pollution should be prevented or reduced at the source wherever feasible;
> ▪ pollution that cannot be prevented should be recycled in an environmentally safe manner whenever feasible;
> ▪ pollution that cannot be prevented or recycled should be treated in an environmentally safe manner whenever feasible; and
> ▪ disposal or other release into the environment should be employed only as a last resort and should be conducted in an environmentally safe manner.

Based on this hierarchy, and subsequent interpretations by the Environmental Protection Agency, the definition of *pollution prevention* has become any effort to reduce the quantity of industrial, hazardous, or toxic waste through changes in the waste-generating or production process *at the source*. Therefore, true pollution prevention encompasses all actions which provide for net reductions in either waste volume or hazard or toxicity taken prior to the waste being generated.

This emphasis on actions taken at the point of pollutant generation implies that end-of-pipe technologies, such as recycling and sludge dewatering, which are applied after the waste has been generated, are not, as defined by the act, pollution prevention practices. However, that should not be taken too literally. Although it is true that postgeneration technologies are not, in the strictest sense, pollution prevention, they are still desirable. The act simply implies there may be better approaches for generators to investigate.

Pollution Prevention Hierarchy

Other authors have recognized the tie between the hierarchy and the variety of waste reduction options available from a technological standpoint. The natural outcome is the fact that some technologies are more desirable than others and should receive greater consideration. Baker, Dunforn, and Warren (1991) proposed the pollution prevention hierarchy shown in Fig. 4-1 with the most desirable options being highest on the hierarchy.

In a vein similar to what is found in the 1990 Pollution Prevention Act, Baker's hierarchy was undoubtedly written in very general terms so it can encompass nearly any pollution prevention or hazardous waste minimization technology and is thereby useful for investigating a wide range of investment possibilities under step 1 of the financial analysis, determining investment alternatives. However, based on the Pollution Prevention Act's narrower definition of *prevention*, the hierarchy can be simplified even further to:

1. *Production process and/or procedure changes.*   Either material substitution—using nonhazardous inputs to the manufacturing process in place of hazardous materials—or an alteration

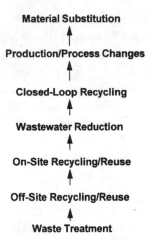

Figure 4-1. Baker's pollution prevention hierarchy.

of the manufacturing or service processes which either reduces the volume or toxicity or completely eliminates the hazardous waste.

2. *Treatment.* All other end-of-pipe methods to include recycling, reuse, and discharge or release of waste for treatment or to the environment.

In interpreting the "worth" of a pollution prevention project, regardless of which hierarchy is used, the higher the potential project is on the hierarchy, the more beneficial the investment should be if all other technological and cost variables are equal.

The requirement to consider these projects in the investment scheme brought out an additional shortfall; the need for hard cost and benefit data for use in justifying pollution prevention investment. This is particularly true with respect to issues such as long-term liability. For example, MacLean (1987a) used the concept of "true" cost of waste disposal in support of pollution prevention projects involving long-term cost reduction to address this information gap. Similar to the tiered costs presented previously, under MacLean's definition, these long-term costs are made up of both direct costs (waste collection, transportation, sampling, and so on) and future liabilities [such as corrective action costs under the Resource Conservation and Recovery Act (RCRA), Superfund-type actions, and third-party lawsuits]. Given the trends in both the tendency to bring suit and the increasing size of the awards in environmental personal injury lawsuits (MacLean 1989), as well as the magnitude of the economic investment required for remediation of hazardous waste spills and sites, the ability to estimate future liability has become one of the major factors in minimizing long-term costs.

Hence, the legal requirement for a strong pollution prevention program within a company was established, and the financial necessity became apparent. To this end, the EPA's Office of Risk Reduction Engineering Laboratory (1992) released its *Facility Pollution Prevention Guide* which has become the standard in establishing a pollution prevention program. However, given that the emphasis of this text is specifically on justifying pollution prevention investment, such management guides will be left for the reader's investigation.

Data Sources

Conversely, there is a specific need, again under step 1 of the financial analysis, to have a method with which to discover pollution prevention investment opportunities. To this end, a number of data sources are available even within the smallest firm. Given that the focus of the Pollution Prevention Act is on hazardous wastes, as defined under RCRA (1986) and CERCLA (1986), a review of the firm's hazardous waste manifests is the logical starting point. These documents will specify the types and volumes of waste that are leaving the firm for treatment or disposal. In general, the majority of the waste should carry the majority of the expense which implies the most opportunistic investment. Similarly, a review of the firm's accounting records will reveal the payees for hazardous waste expenses again leading to opportunistic investments.

There are other databases in existing firms that, although not financially oriented, could reveal investment opportunities. For example, a review of the data reported under the requirements of the toxic release inventory (TRI) will likewise reveal the types of hazardous waste both sent for treatment and disposal as well as released to the environment. These data can be invaluable to uncovering pollution prevention investment opportunities for wastes that are not currently regulated as hazardous as well as for upcoming environmental compliance requirements. For example, many of the regulatory requirements being codified by the EPA from the latest reauthorization of the Clean Air Act allow for a phase-in date. Given that a firm may not have been regulated for particular emissions in the past, the TRI data will show where reductions can be made in view of future compliance requirements.

Another source of data is the results of either internal or external compliance assessments. Although many of the assessment reports do not contain specific volumes of waste released or treated, they do indicate compliance problem areas. A specific benefit of pollution prevention is the potential to eliminate compliance problems. For example, if a firm is experiencing compliance problems with the release of volatile organic compounds (VOCs), a logical pollution prevention investment would be to substitute a non-VOC solvent in the process (material substitution) or move to an abrasive procedure such as bead blasting (process change), both pollution prevention alternatives, to help solve the compliance problem.

At the end of the data search phase, most firms will probably have far more potential projects than resources. Hence, once pollution prevention alternatives have been discovered, there must be some way to "rack and stack" the different opportunities. Although the availability of specific technologies may seem like a logical first cut to investment, it may lead to less desirable investment opportunities. For example, there may be technologies readily available to reduce or eliminate the quantity of waste X released by a firm. However, if the firm spends only a small fraction of its environmental budget due to emissions of X, it may not be the best starting point from the standpoint of economic benefit. To this end, the first logical step in laying out the firm's investment strategy should be to rank-order the waste by cost to the firm. In this manner, the best investment opportunities become relatively apparent; the wastes generated which have the largest financial impact should be those with the biggest potential for return. Under this first-cut rack-and-stack method, the high payoff potential projects will naturally be at the top of the opportunities list.

Ranking potential projects in this manner has an additional benefit. The projects with the highest payback to the firm can be looked upon as low-hanging fruit. Especially if a firm is just beginning its pollution prevention efforts, showing success in the first few projects could be key to maintaining management's financial interest. In addition, if there are substantial savings from the first investments, the monies "saved" can be looked upon as a bank to finance additional efforts. In this manner, a successful program can actually grow on its own accord by reinvesting its savings within the program. Then, once the listing of opportunities has been established, these most opportunistic waste streams can be compared to available technologies with emphasis on both mass and toxicity reduction.

Once technically sound pollution prevention alternatives have been found, step 2 in the financial analysis, determining the variables to be included in the analysis, can begin. Thus far in the text we have assumed that there would be no change in production levels for the life of the project. However, that assumption is neither realistic nor desirable in most cases. The production schedule for the majority of firms includes either growth or plans for potential scalebacks; downsizing or upsizing. Even in relatively stable situations, few firms don't experience natural highs and lows in the business cycle such as the gain and loss of clients and seasonal growth patterns. Given that one of the major factors which can influence the pollution prevention investment decision is waste disposal costs, a method to tie production to waste generation must be established to account for changing production rates.

Predicting Hazardous Waste Generation

In an organizational method similar to that discussed in Sec. 2, the first step in the process of tying production to waste generation is to establish both baseline and variable pollutant releases.

For example, in a typical firm an example of a baseline waste could be fly ash from the firm's boilers. Regardless of the production levels, the heating plant must be operated as long as the firm is open. Hence, the volume of fly ash would be considered as a baseline cost because, short of adding or eliminating a shift of workers, its volume is not generally tied to production levels.

Similarly, other constant pollutant releases such as renewing solvent dip tanks or evaporation from plating baths which can be considered more or less the emissions resulting from having the door open for business should all be included in this baseline. This is not to say that these wastes cannot be reduced; however, because they are not tied to production levels within the firm, they need to be classified separately as baseline wastes.

Conversely, a number of pollutant emissions can be directly tied to a firm's production. For example, there should be a direct relationship between the amount of cadmium-bearing wastewater and the volume of dragout from the parts plated in the cadmium-plating bath; it should be possible to tie the volume of waste paint stripper directly to the number of parts processed. These variable waste generations are dealt with in the same manner as an accountant would handle variable costs in determining the cost of a final product. Once established, these data form the baseline to predicting the volumes and/or masses of waste produced in day-to-day operations at the firm and will be used to project future waste generation as a result of production changes.

From a retrospective standpoint, changes in waste volume and/or mass are easy to determine. One simply needs to compare the wastes generated in the current year (X) to those generated in the previous year $(X - 1)$. The units can be any convenient variable: drums, pounds, gallons, and so on. If there is less volume, it could indicate that pollution prevention efforts are working. However, although this measurement is direct and easy to understand, it can be misleading. For example, if 1200 pounds of a specific pollutant were generated in the current year and only 1000 pounds had been generated in the previous year, it would imply that the pollution prevention investment had not been beneficial; more pollutants had been generated. However, if production during the same time period was increased 50 percent, the 20 percent increase in pollutant generation could actually represent a net decrease in pollutant per unit of production; pollution prevention investment would have been effective. Conversely, had there been a reduction in the previous year's 1000 pounds of pollutant generated to 750 pounds, but at the same time the firm suffered a 50 percent drop in production, the 250-pound pollutant reduction would actually mean that the "rate" of generation of the pollutant increased. Hence, these variable generations must be tied to production in some sort of rate expression.

Indexing

The first method to tie the generation of pollutants to production is referred to as *indexing*. This method is based on the ratio of the production activity during one period to that of another. This expression of production is referred to as the *activity index*. Because this method is tied directly to production, it only works well for variable waste generation and for predicting the potential changes in disposal costs. However, if the purpose of the analysis was the prediction of the total waste disposal charges in the future for the firm, the effects of baseline waste generation could be included in the analysis.

The computation of the index is straightforward, any convenient unit can be used, e.g., gallons, drums, kilograms, and cubic yards, and the index can be easily projected to expected production levels in the future. Its computation merely requires taking the production in a year in which the waste generation is known and dividing that figure into the predicted level of production for the year in question. This results in an activity index specific to the production line and product. To compute projected waste generation, the activity index can then be multiplied by the waste generated in the baseline year, and the result is the expected volume of waste in the out-years as follows:

$$\text{Index} = \frac{\text{production}_{\text{year } X}}{\text{production}_{\text{year } Y}}$$

$$\text{Waste}_{\text{year } X} = \text{index}_{\frac{\text{year } X}{\text{year } Y}} \times \text{waste}_{\text{year } Y}$$

In the most simplistic terms, this method assumes that the result of doubling production would be to double the variable waste generated by the production activity, i.e., next year's production divided by this year's production = 2, then next year's waste generation should also be twice as high.

To show how activity indexing works in a slightly more complex example, assume that the electronics firm which we have investigated in previous examples produced 100,000 circuit boards in generating the 3950 gallons of waste shown in the baseline mass balance diagram in Fig. 3-2. Further, instead of using the constant production assumption, presume that over the 10-year analysis, interviews with the firm's sales force showed that a number of contracts were either expiring or starting as follows:

- A current contract will end in 1 year with a reduction in production of 15,000 units per year.

- A new contract will begin in 2 years, last for 5 years, and increase production by 20,000 units per year.

- An additional current contract will end in 3 years with a reduction in production of 10,000 units per year.

- A second new contract will begin in 5 years, last for 4 years, and increase production by 35,000 units per year.

- A third new contract will start in 6 years, last for 5 years, and increase production by 10,000 units per year.

The effects of these varying production levels on waste generation can be easily accounted for with indexing. The first step is to show these changes in production from the baseline. Again, for simplicity, it shall be assumed that each contract will start and end at the beginning or end of a year; however, the midyear contracts could easily be included. For the first year, the production will drop from 100,000 units processed to 85,000. Hence, the activity index would be 85,000/100,000 or 0.85. This implies the waste production for the next year should be 85 percent of the current year or 0.85 × 3950 gallons = 3360 gallons (again, only three significant figures are used). The disposal cost due to variable wastes for next year could then be computed as 3360 gal-

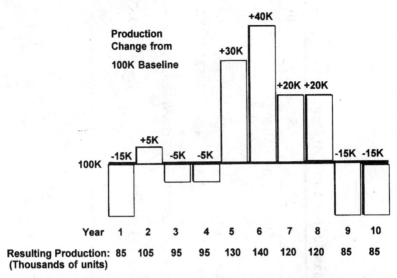

Figure 4-2. Production change time line for the electronics firm.

lons × $2.50/gallon = $8400 if the prices were constant. At the selected price increase of 5 percent due to inflation and a 4 percent real price increase, the cost of waste disposal in the next year would be 1.09 × $8400 = $9150. Similarly, production could be estimated for the entire 10-year period as shown in Fig. 4-2.

From the data supplied by the production time line, it is a simple matter to compute the activity index as well as the projected waste production and cost. These figures are shown in Table 4-1.

From the table the expected volume of waste produced as well as the costs for waste disposal are readily computed, and, if a spreadsheet is used, changes are easily accomplished. In investigating the pollution prevention options such as the business-as-usual versus recycle versus material substitution example done in the previous chapter, tables similar to 4-1 could easily be established for all the variable inputs such as the amount of new solvent purchased for all the pollution prevention options investigated.

Herein lies the first limitation to using the method of indexing. Unless specifically addressed, the method assumes that all waste

Table 4-1. Activity Indexing for the Electronics Firm—Baseline of 100,000 Units

Year	0	1	2	3	4	5	6	7	8	9	10
Annual production (from Fig. 4-2, thousands)	100	85	105	95	95	130	140	120	120	85	85
Activity index	1	0.85	1.05	0.95	0.95	1.3	1.4	1.2	1.2	0.85	0.85
Resulting waste, gallons	3950	3357.5	4147.5	3752.5	3752.5	5135	5530	4740	4740	3357.5	3357.5
Disposal costs (at $2.50)	$9,875	$8,394	$10,369	$9,381	$9,381	$12,838	$13,825	$11,850	$11,850	$8,394	$8,394
Disposal costs (with inflation and real price increases)		$9,149	$12,319	$12,149	$13,242	$19,752	$23,186	$21,662	$23,612	$18,230	$19,871

produced is production related. Hence, if any portion of the 3950 gallons of waste was related to the baseline cost of doing business as discussed earlier, that portion would have to be subtracted from the baseline before the activity index was applied. The calculations would then be performed as before up to the point of computing the cost of waste disposal. If the analysis were being performed to show the change in cost from business as usual, the baseline waste generation would not need to be included. However, if the analysis were being performed as part of a tasking to predict the total waste generation or total waste disposal costs over the future, the baseline waste volume or mass would be included before computing the total waste cost.

The second limitation to indexing is that the method has the built-in assumption that the waste generation is linearly related to production. This assumption leads to two shortcomings. First, the assumption implies that if production is doubled or halved, waste generation will likewise be doubled or halved, which may not always be the case. For example, in an electroplating operation, parts are first dipped in a bath which affixes the plating metal electrochemically. When the proper coverage has been applied, the parts are then rinsed in a water tank and sent on for machining, packaging, shipment, and so on. The rinse tank has a water supply to ensure that the concentration of metal from the bath remains below a specified limit. The linear assumption in the indexing method implies that if two parts are plated, the resulting waste generated will be double that generated if only one part were plated. However, the rinse tank may have only one flow rate or a limited number of flow rates to keep the plating solution from concentrating metal ions in the rinse water. Hence, if parts were rinsed one at a time, the linear relationship assumed within the method would be valid; as each part is rinsed, a set volume of water would be used to maintain the rinse tank. Conversely, if two parts were rinsed at the same time, given that the measure of waste production used is rinse water volume, the linear relationship could be lost.

Second, this assumption further implies that the waste generated per part produced is constant over time, e.g., doubling or halving the number of parts will likewise double or halve the waste generated. Although this could hold true for long production runs of the same or very similar items, it can lead to inaccuracies. For example, consider normal maintenance on an aircraft which would include stripping and cleaning the old finish and repainting the outer surface. If the production unit used in computing the activity index were an aircraft, the measure could be misleading. For example, in considering military aircraft, if only F-15 fighters, or aircraft of a similar size such as F-16 fighters, were serviced by a facility, the index of waste per fighter could be valid. However, if both small fighter aircraft (such as the F-15) and large cargo transports (such as the C-5A Galaxy) were both serviced by the same facility, the linearity of the relationship between the volume or mass of waste generated and the number of aircraft serviced would be invalid. These limitations to indexing method lead to another option in measuring pollution prevention, the throughput ratio.

Throughput Ratio

The theory underlying the throughput ratio is very similar to that underlying the concept of mass balance. Unlike indexing, which uses the production unit as the basis of prediction, with throughput ratio the waste volume or mass generated is related to the amount of the new chemical used in the operation; that is, the ratio of the mass of the chemical contained in the waste to the mass of the chemical input to the process is a measurement of the mass of the chemical that was used in the process. The lower the throughput ratio (i.e., the lower the mass of input chemical that ends up in the waste), the more efficient the operation.

While this may seem like a more accurate measurement method, it does have the limitation that it cannot distinguish between use and loss. For example, if the main purpose of the operation is to convert input to product, the throughput ratio would indicate the efficiency of the operation in that it would represent how much of the input material ended up in the waste; however, it would not provide any information regarding material lost due to evaporation, spills, and so on. For example, if one measured the quantity of plating metal in the rinse water for an electroplating operation and divided it by the amount of chemical added, the result would be an indicator of how much metal was lost in the rinse water, but the measure would not distinguish between the metal actually plated on parts and the metal lost through spills, lost as the part is machined, and so on.

This limitation not withstanding, throughput ratio can be a used as a predictor for future waste generation given two assumptions. First, unless there is a process change, it must be assumed that the throughput ratio will be constant over time except for the effect of the number of units produced; if the efficiency of the production operation is changed, the throughput ratio will likewise have to be recalculated. Second, as was the case in indexing, the amount of input chemical must be directly proportional and linearly related to the production. If these assumptions can be made, throughput ratio can be used to predict future waste generation by simply multiplying the throughput ratio by the amount of input material projected to be used:

$$\text{Throughput ratio} = \frac{\text{amount of chemical}_{\text{waste}}}{\text{amount of chemical}_{\text{input}}}$$

$$\text{Waste}_{\text{year X}} = \text{throughput ratio} \times \text{input}_{\text{year X}}$$

Again taking the electronics firm as an example, the next year's waste generation would be computed by first taking the 3950 gallons of solvent in the waste and dividing it by the 4000 gallons of solvent input to the system. The result would be a throughput ratio of 0.9875. Then, the assumption must be made that since production would drop 15 percent in the next year so would the volume of solvent input to the system. Hence, the solvent used in the next year would be 85 percent of the current year's use, or 3400 gallons. Applying the throughput ratio to this projected solvent use would yield the waste solvent expected to be generated: 0.9875 × 3400 gallons = 3360 gallons—the same value obtained in the indexing method.

To aid in computations, a solvent input time line similar to Fig. 4-2 can be established (see Fig. 4-3). As before, the computations for throughput ratio and projected waste volumes and costs, as shown in Table 4-2, are simplified by making the time line.

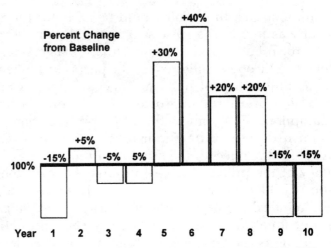

Year	1	2	3	4	5	6	7	8	9	10
Projected Solvent Use: (4,000-gallon baseline)	3360	4150	3750	3750	5140	5530	4740	4740	3360	3360

Figure 4-3. Solvent input time line for the electronics firm.

Although throughput ratio may seem like a rather tedious way to predict waste generation in that it encompasses many of the same computations as indexing, it can be ideal depending upon the information available within the firm. In the case of the electronics firm in the above examples, the activity index may be the preferred method because the firm's endpoint was a service, a clean circuit board, instead of a product. In cases such as paint manufacture where the majority of the input goes into the final product, throughput ratio man be an ideal measure. This is especially true if the production personnel within the firm can provide not only production figures but projected input materials. In this case, the throughput ratio could be directly applied, avoiding having to compute production changes as an interim step.

The largest potential pitfall from both of the methods examined above is that they do not take toxicity of the waste into account. For example, both zinc and cadmium have been used as a protective coating to inhibit corrosion on metals for many years. It would not be difficult to find an example where, based on analyses performed on throughput ratio or indexing, the conclusion could be drawn that switching to cadmium could be

Table 4-2. Throughput Ratio for the Electronics Firm—Baseline of 100,000 Units

Year	1	2	3	4	5	6	7	8	9	10
Projected solvent use, gallons (from Fig. 4-3)	3,400	4,200	3,800	3,800	5,200	5,600	4,800	4,800	3,400	3,400
Throughput ratio (3950 gallons/4000 gallons)	0.9875	0.9875	0.9875	0.9875	0.9875	0.9875	0.9875	0.9875	0.9875	0.9875
Resulting waste, gallons (measured from baseline)	3,358	4,148	3,753	3,753	5,135	5,530	4,740	4,740	3,358	3,358
Disposal costs	$8,394	$10,369	$9,381	$9,381	$12,838	$13,825	$11,850	$11,850	$8,394	$8,394
Disposal costs (with inflation and real price increases)	$9,149	$12,319	$12,149	$13,242	$19,752	$23,186	$21,662	$23,612	$18,230	$19,871

an advantage in terms of the mass of waste generated. Unfortunately, the fact that cadmium is far more toxic than zinc could be the most important factor to consider in the analysis and would be overlooked in such volume- or mass-centered computations.

Similarly, indexing and throughput ratio analyses performed as above which show potential reductions in the generation of waste do not indicate potential problems due to changing the media which receives the waste. For example, if a firm were to switch from a liquid-based cadmium electroplating operation to a vapor-coating system, even though there would probably be far less waste and far less disposal cost, if the receiving media were the air versus a liquid waste stream, the effect in terms of the extent of human and/or environmental exposure could be important. Although these topics are beyond the scope of this text, they are important variables and must be considered in any such analysis.

In addition to the requirement to predict the volumes of waste which will be generated, the indexing and throughput ratio methods outlined above can serve to measure the actual results of pollution prevention efforts retrospectively. Such analyses should be performed both to ensure that the investment is paying off as expected and to verify the validity of the chosen method. Both methods are flexible enough to easily allow for comparisons of the current year's waste generation to either the previous year or to a specific baseline year depending upon the goals established with the firm's pollution prevention program.

Appendix 4A   Estimating Long-Term Cleanup Liability

As implied throughout this text, the critical element which determines the success or failure of a pollution prevention investment is whether "the numbers work." If a project cannot be justified on a financial basis, it often has little chance of being implemented. Fortunately, a number of pollution prevention investments can be justified on the basis of direct, easily measured costs; however, issues such as remediation under the

Comprehensive Environmental Response, Compensation, and Liability Act (CERCLA), Resource Conservation and Recovery Act (RCRA) cleanup actions, and so on, while harder to predict, could become the driving force behind the investment decision once there is no more low-hanging fruit.

To show how the subjects discussed in the text can be used to help solve common financial problems, an investigation, taken from Aldrich (1992), used to predict one of these "potential, future liability" costs is presented. Given that this is only a summary of the referenced work, some of the detail presented herein would be either implied or omitted in reality, and where details were unimportant for this example they were omitted. Further, this example is not meant to be the only interpretation of the legal requirements nor should the probabilities, discount rates, and so on used here be taken as the only possible variable values. Instead, this example is presented to demonstrate how the microeconomic principles, engineering economic equations, accounting classifications, and uncertainty can be combined in a more complex analysis.

Defining Consumer Surplus in the Landfill Industry

To examine the effect of landfill disposal on consumer surplus and therefore determine whether there is an externality, one of the first steps is to establish the supply and demand functions for landfills. However, if the microeconomic theory developed thus far in the text is extended to landfills, a problem arises. The demand curve previously presented represents the aggregate of all individual consumer demands. Fortunately, with few exceptions, consumers, i.e., the individual purchasers of goods and services, do not consume or use hazardous waste landfill services directly. As a result, a derived demand relationship can be developed which represents a summation of individual consumer demand.

The demand for landfill space is a result of the demand for waste disposal by firms or industries which generate hazardous waste through the production of products and services. Although measuring this waste generator's demand is not a "pure" demand relationship—it is not a direct summation of all the individual consumer demands—it will serve well as a valid proxy if it can be shown that it mirrors the individual consumer's demand. This similarity in relationship can be done with one assumption: Firms or industries which generate hazardous waste as a by-product in their production of goods and services must pass the cost of hazardous waste disposal onto the consumer via product price. In other words, the firms must recover their production costs over the long term to make a profit and thereby remain in business. As a result, the cost of landfilling waste as well as any other production cost must ultimately be borne by the consumer. Therefore, in consuming a product or a service from a successful firm or industry, consumers are essentially showing their preference for, or at least acceptance of, the firm's waste disposal practices. Hence, if the firm disposes of waste in a landfill, it is a result of the consumer's demand for the goods or services offered; consumer and producer (waste generator) demand for landfill space must be synonymous.

Although a few refinements can be made, because the supply and demand functions for hazardous waste landfills are governed by the same laws of supply and demand, their general shape must be similar to those shown in the hypothetical example in Fig. 1-1. Looking first at the demand function, under the law of demand, if the price of landfill disposal were reduced, more waste would be landfilled. In this specific case, this is because lowered landfill costs would mean that fewer waste minimization or pollution prevention efforts would be profitable, and more landfill space would be demanded. Likewise, if landfill tipping fees were increased, more such efforts would be financially attractive. This gives the demand function for landfills the typical negative slope. However, because there are alternatives to using landfills to dispose of waste, there is an implied price ceiling or maximum cost on how much can be charged, namely, the price of alternative disposal technologies. For example, if the landfill price were increased to the point where it equalled or were higher than competitive technologies (e.g., incineration), waste generators would shift their demand for landfills to the other, less expensive disposal technologies, and there would be no demand for landfilling waste. Hence, with respect to demand, the above analysis implies there is a maximum price that can be charged, and demand will increase as prices are lowered.

With respect to the supply function, the uniqueness of the landfill industry imposes a time sensitivity which governs the quantity of landfill service that can be supplied. As explained earlier, changes in the supply function can only be caused by changes in the supply parameters. For example, when entrepreneurs move into or out of a business endeavor, the supply parameter "number of suppliers" changes, which causes the supply of a good or service to increase or decrease. However, this movement into and out of a specific industry assumes that entrepreneurs are free to move their capital into and out of the industry. In the case of the hazardous waste landfill industry, this may not be an easy task. Because of environmental permits, public opposition, and so on, in addition to the normal construction and production time requirements, constructing and starting a landfill can be and normally is a long and expensive process. In addition, because environmental regulations require separate permits both to build and to operate landfills, merely shifting resources into the landfill industry does not even guarantee the entrepreneur will be able to operate the landfill, thereby changing the supply parameter.

Similarly, if an entrepreneur wishes to exit the landfill market, the mere fact that the landfill is closed and will no longer accept waste does not release the entrepreneur's resources for other endeavors. Instead, not only does financial liability for closure actions such as capping and long-term ground-water monitoring remain with the entrepreneur, the land itself is unavailable for other uses. As a result, over the period required to site, permit, build, and start to accept waste at a new landfill (easily 8 to 10 years), the ability of the industry to increase either the number of landfills or the available volume in their current landfills is limited. This leads to an implied maximum landfill supply, Q_{max}. At levels less than Q_{max}, the landfill supply can be only affected by opening additional cells within the existing landfills. Hence, the analysis dictates that the supply function must follow the law of supply with the exception that there is an implied maximum quantity which can be supplied to the market.

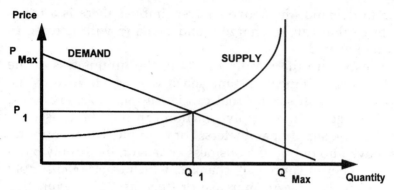

Figure 4-4. The supply-demand relationship for landfills.

To show these specific stipulations graphically, the supply and demand functions for landfills as postulated are shown in Fig. 4-4. The price P_{max} reflects the cost of competing technologies and represents the maximum price that suppliers could charge for landfill services. Similarly, the near vertical portion of the supply function reflects Q_{max}, the maximum volume available to those demanding services from the landfill industry. As drawn, waste producers would dispose Q_1 units at the given unit price of P_1.

Even though the shape of the supply and demand function postulated in Fig. 4-4 varies from the hypothetical model, the measure of consumer surplus remains straightforward and can be graphically represented as in Fig. 4-5, which again is keyed to

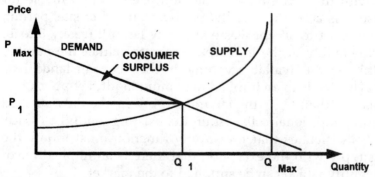

Figure 4-5. Consumer surplus in the landfill industry.

the point of intersection of the supply and demand functions. As shown in the figure, the existence of consumer surplus can be readily identified, and, as before, any increases or decreases in consumer surplus from this baseline can be used to indicate changes in consumer or social welfare.

Defining the Landfill Industry Externality

There are many sources of potential financial liability associated with landfilling hazardous waste which, presumably, could lead to negative externalities: corrective actions under the Resource Conservation and Recovery Act (RCRA) and third-party lawsuits for personal/property damages under the Comprehensive Environmental Response Compensation and Liability Act (CERCLA) are just two. The existence of any such externality would tend to decrease consumer surplus as shown in Fig. 1-14. However, to simplify this analysis, this text shall only consider one potential liability: the cost involved in destroying the waste. Destruction of the waste was selected as the key variable because destruction eliminates any further financial liability for the waste generator (i.e., the individual who generated the waste and disposed of same in the landfill). Further, this simplification restricts the analysis to a single, relatively predictable cost. Other associated "cleanup" costs such as excavation; overburden, which likewise must be disposed of; sampling and analysis; and so on are variable and based on site-specific parameters. Further, this simplification has a valuable benefit in the business world. In that it tends to underestimate versus overestimate long-term liability, there is less potential for management to allege that the cost savings projected from a pollution prevention investment was artificially high.

This analysis begins with the technical parameters of the landfill design. Current landfill design requirements, as outlined by RCRA, include both earthen and synthetic liner systems, leak detection, leachate collection systems, and so on. Although these design requirements serve well as additional safeguards to better contain the waste, if one accepts the fact that all humanmade structures will eventually fail, these design improvements do not totally eliminate potential failure. Instead, the design criterion tends to limit the potential for uncontrolled and/or undetected problems, thereby only reducing the magnitude of the potential financial liability of landfill failure instead of eliminating the possibility. Modern landfill design notwithstanding, once failure occurs, the site will have to be remediated. This implies that there will always be the requirement for waste destruction, either upon generation of the waste or during remediation of the landfill. Hence, the cost of destroying the waste has become the focus of this study.

Based on the arguments presented above, all landfills, modern, RCRA facilities included, will fail at some time in the future. This inevitable failure implies the landfill fees paid at the time of disposal represent little more than storage charges. Firms who only incorporate the tipping fee into their analyses are ignoring additional financial liability for waste destruction which should be considered and added to the cost of disposal. In that users of landfills generally ignore waste destruction in computing the cost of waste disposal, this cost of destruction for the waste would appear to be a negative externality.

Social Cost Analysis

The social cost of the landfill externality can be added to the landfill supply and demand graph previously shown in Fig. 4-5. The social cost (P_s) is the present value of the future destruction cost and should be added to the supply function for landfills as shown in Fig. 4-6.

As before, in considering the social cost, the amount of waste sent to the landfill should be limited to Q_f versus Q_1, and the price charged should be P_f. As shown in Sec. 1, the addition of social cost reduces the actual consumer surplus from landfilling as compared to that reflected in the market by just the landfill price. Instead of the area below the demand function and above the price P_1, it is actually the area below the demand function and above P_f. Destruction costs are inherent to the generation of hazardous waste, and if this cost is not accounted for in the price structure of the landfill market, it implies that there is an external or societal cost of production.

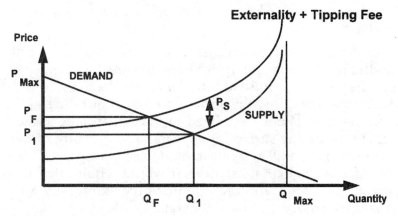

Figure 4-6. The landfill externality.

Because the life of the landfill (i.e., time to failure) is so long, expressing the magnitude of this externality as a present value cost becomes a problem in dealing with the time value of money. If there were a zero discount rate, it would imply that the cost of destroying the waste in the future would be the same as the cost of destruction at today's price. Therefore, at a zero discount rate, the total cost of disposing of one unit of waste (P_t) would be the landfill price (P_l) plus the social cost (P_s) as represented by the current unit price of the alternative, destruction technology.

Assuming positive discount rates (it is doubtful that banks will ever pay consumers to borrow money), there are two possible scenarios concerning the present value of future waste destruction. First, if the cost of waste destruction remained constant over the period in question, the positive discount rate would imply that the present value of the cost of destroying the waste at a future date would be less than the current destruction price, i.e., payments received in the future have lower present values given positive discount rates. Conversely, if the combined effects of inflation and real price increases were greater than the discount rate, the present value of the future expenditure could be higher than current price. Under either scenario, however, there would still be a social cost to consider.

Landfill Negative
Externality Analysis

As demonstrated in Sec. 1, because of the existence of a social cost, landfilling waste is underpriced and too great a quantity is sent for disposal. To those waste generators which do not include destruction costs, the social cost does not represent a direct expense and is not considered in their financial decision making. Hence, on the surface, it appears to be a failure of the market to internalize all relevant costs to the generator of the waste. Under normal circumstances, it would require that the government pass legislation to eliminate the externality and internalize this cost for the waste generators.

There are two general market intervention options that can be used by the government to eliminate the externality. The first would be for the government to directly limit the amount of waste that is allowed to be sent to landfills. Such emission limitations are the basis of the Clean Air and Clean Water Acts. The second regulatory option would be to force an increase in the cost of disposal.

Under the first scenario, emission limits, if the amount of waste allowed to be sent for disposal were limited to Q_f as shown in Fig. 4-6, either by issuing or selling disposal permits or assuming a command and control position on hazardous waste "emissions," the quantity of waste landfilled would be correctly set.

Conversely, emission limits could be achieved if the price of waste disposal, as seen by the generator of the waste, were increased from P_1 to P_f by a tax or fee levied on the generator of the waste. This price increase would raise the disposal cost, which would also have the effect of limiting the quantity of waste sent to disposal to the correct amount. Either option would force waste generators to consider the "total" cost (P_l + P_s) for waste disposal in their market decisions.

The above government options share one major assumption, namely, that a negative externality actually exists *which requires* additional regulatory intervention. Although most waste generators routinely do not include destruction costs in their price analyses of landfill disposal, it is not certain that this is a result of market failure, and, therefore, the situation may not require additional legislation to be corrected. Instead, the apparent externality is a failure of the generators to recognize the total costs associated with their waste disposal options. This could be caused by a lack of understanding of the legal requirements, a consideration of only the short-term profit versus the long-term responsibility, a feeling of financial security in that the waste was handled "correctly" under current environmental law, or the inability of the generator to estimate the magnitude of this cost.

In any event, the present environmental laws (RCRA and CERCLA) already designate the party generating the waste as the financially responsible party. Therefore, if it can be shown that the market has the capability to internalize these costs, no further legislative intervention is required. Under the Resource Conservation and Recovery Act, the generator of the waste (or consumer of landfill services) is financially liable for the waste from "cradle to grave." Although this seems to imply that once the waste is in a landfill, the RCRA "grave" has been attained, the waste producer's financial liability for the waste does not end. The Comprehensive Environmental Response, Compensation and Liability Act (CERCLA) [as amended by the Superfund Amendments and Reauthorization Act (SARA)] extends this liability for as long as the waste exists.

In defining this legal responsibility for generators of hazardous waste, the laws define two concepts of liability. The first, joint and several liability, allows the EPA to assign the full financial liability for destruction of *all* waste in a landfill to any generator who has deposited waste at the facility. Hence, in the strictest sense, any generator who has deposited waste in a landfill can be legally held financially liable for the entire cost of a landfill remediation. The second concept, strict liability, limits the government's requirements in proving the waste generator's "guilt" in the event of environmental damage. Under strict liability, in a landfill situation, the only issues that a government agency such as the EPA needs to prove in order to assign financial liability are whether the environment was damaged, to what extent it was damaged, and the identity of the owner of the landfilled waste. Circumstances that may otherwise be considered extenuating, such as recent changes in the prevailing regulations or the state-of-the-art technologies that were available at the time of disposal, are irrelevant and need not be considered in assigning financial responsibility. Hence, the requirement to address issues such as intent to commit environmental harm, negligence in waste disposal, and so on are eliminated by the law.

The net effect of the current hazardous waste legislation is clear: The waste producer's financial liability exists as long as the waste exists. As a result, to internalize this cost, it only is required that this financial responsibility be communicated to waste generators, not the passage of further legislation. As shown earlier, defining this cost through microeconomic theory (i.e., determine the cost of P_s from Fig. 4-6) is valid and forms the basis of this analysis.

Landfill Failure Analysis

A landfill is considered to be a containment vessel for hazardous waste. Hence, failure can simply be defined as the time when the vessel no longer contains the waste. Given the current landfill design criteria, the critical failure variable is the liner system. If the primary liner fails and excessive waste is detected in the leachate collection system between the liners, the landfill will have failed, and remediation will be required.

This approach may seem to negate site factors such as soil permeability, contaminant transport, adsorption, and the like which could affect leachate flow; however, these concepts are relevant to an exposure risk analysis centering on the receptor such as would be performed in a remediation under CERCLA. Because CERCLA specifically addresses the potential for uncontrolled releases of contaminants to the environment from sites no longer in service, such as the abandoned Love Canal landfill, the law must be primarily concerned with controlling exposure to the receptor. Conversely, RCRA addresses treatment, storage, and disposal facilities for hazardous waste generated during current operations. As such, it must emphasize the facility versus the potential exposure to the receptor. This means that the requirement for remediation under RCRA would be determined solely by the performance of the facility (i.e., the capability of the landfill to contain the waste), and site-specific variables such as soil permeability would not enter into the remediation decision. Hence, the time to landfill failure can be defined by the time to liner failure.

There are and have been a number of studies regarding landfill liner failure; however, they are often simulations of landfill conditions done in a laboratory. For example, EPA's Test Method 9090 (1984) involves testing the actual (or simulated) waste compatibility with the liner in a laboratory over months. Whereas the results of such simulations are valuable, they are of limited use in defining the actual time to landfill failure due to the number of potential variables that occur in an actual landfill.

Conversely, there has been one very comprehensive in situ effort (Bonaparte and Gross 1990) which studied field data on leachate flows detected by the leakage detection layers of double-liner systems at 30 landfills. The most critical aspect of this study is that all the landfills investigated were designed to the specifications required by the 1984 Hazardous and Solid Waste Amendments to RCRA.

Included in the study are data on leachate flow measurements taken at three specific times: the end of construction where consolidation water, secondary compression of the clay liners, and so on are critical aspects of leachate flow; during landfill operation; and during the postoperational phases. During the operational period, the study included 109 separate flow measurements taken on 50 separate landfill cells. The flow rate data from the study is broken down in Table 4-3.

Judging from the data presented by Bonaparte, it is apparent that landfills "leak." The critical aspect to defining landfill failure therefore becomes a complex question. First, what would

Table 4-3. Average Leachate Flows from 50 Individual Landfill Cells (in liters per hectare per day)*

0 < cell flow < 50	50 < cell flow < 200	200 < cell flow
18	19	13

*Table data reflect final flow rates measured during study (e.g., if flow measurements were taken at 1, 12, 23, and 33 months, only the 33-month measurement is reflected in the table data).

the regulators consider to be an "excessive" leak which would require remediation? Second, will the regulators still consider the landfill to have failed if the leachate collection system can recover the leachate? Third, if an "excessive" flow occurs, to whom will the regulators assign liability for the landfill remediation?

With respect to excessive flows, Bonaparte and Gross (1990) report that the U.S. EPA has proposed "action leakage rates" between 50 and 200 liters per hectare of lined area per day (lphd) as measured by the volume removed by the leachate collection system. Given this possible action level of 50 lphd, over 60 percent of the landfill cells measured in Bonaparte and Gross's study, reflected in Table 4-3, would legally be considered as failed landfills.

The question then arises as to whether the landfill will be considered as failed if the leachate collection system has the capacity to contain the leachate flow. Given the intent of the landfill design criterion, to protect ground-water supplies, there is little doubt that failure of the primary containment barrier will be sufficient to warrant remediation. This assumption is based on two major factors. First, there is no system similar to the leachate collection system to detect or control leakage through the secondary liner (the liner under the leachate collection system) save ground-water monitoring wells. Hence, a leak in the second liner would not be detected until after the damage to the environment had already occurred. Second, the purpose of double liners is similar to that of double-hulled oil tankers for ocean shipment of crude oil. The second liner is a backup to the primary containment system. Allowing a landfill to continue operation with a primary liner leaking would be the same as allowing a double-hulled oil tanker to continue in operation with only one hull intact. As a result, even though the landfill may still potentially be containing the waste, there is little doubt, given the orientation of the regulations to the facility and the intent of the design criteria, that primary liner failure will be synonymous with landfill failure from a regulatory standpoint.

The answer to the question as to who could be held liable for payment in the event of failure lies within the existing regulations. Under the concept of "cradle to grave," waste responsibility was established. The landfill was merely a holding area, and the waste owner is financially responsible for the waste for as long as it exists.

The critical question hence becomes not one of whether or not a landfill will fail but rather when failure will occur, i.e., at what landfill age. In the past, the EPA has been cited as expecting most landfill liners to fail after approximately 20 years (McHugh 1990). This failure age has been argued as being both too long (failure can be accelerated by contact with chlorinated organic solvents in the landfill or exposure to ultraviolet light, and so on) and too short (once in a stable environment there is no driving force to alter the liner, and it should remain stable for decades). However, the 20-year figure has been used in this analysis because it coincides with most liner manufacturers' warrantee period (Hovater 1989). Conversely, given the 24-month average age of the landfill cells in the Bonaparte and Gross study, with a range of 1 to 52 months since the onset of operations, the 20-year lifetime expectation used in this analysis would seem to be somewhat optimistic.

As explained by Hovater (1989) the general wording of liner warranties indicates they are often prorated, and the manufacturer can normally only be held financially responsible for the liner system if the problem is related to defects in materials or work in the liner itself. If the excess leachate detected in the liner system is due to a failure caused either by or during installation (such as leaking seams, construction damage, and so on) rather than in the liner itself, the liner manufacturer would not be held financially responsible. The firm installing the liner would have had to issue a separate warrantee regarding installation defects. Individual warranties and guarantees vary very little, and they all have the common denominator that they are limited in coverage and, except in specific circumstances, probably would not cover full remediation costs. Hence, warranties cannot be considered as financial fail-safes.

Landfill regulations require consideration of an additional variable. Namely, if an excessive leachate flow occurs, what actions will be required? Whereas this is open to conjecture, if liner leaks can be found and isolated, repairs would probably be allowed. In these cases, if the leaks can be attributed to either the failure of a guaranteed liner or warranted installation problems, the waste generators should not be held responsible for repair cost. However, given the limitations on liner warranties, it is doubtful that the liner manufacturer's or installer's compensation would include costs attributed to destroying the waste removed from the landfill in the repair process. Hence, if the leachate flow rates were high enough to preclude repair or if the repair process required that waste be removed from the landfill and treated versus being returned to the landfill, the waste generator, under RCRA and CERCLA liability rules, could be held responsible for the destruction costs.

Because the purpose of this analysis is the financial responsibility for remediation versus an analysis of landfill liner failure, microeconomic theory can again be used to justify the 20-year life selected for this study. This is based on two assumptions. First, most "early leaks" (such as reflected in the Bonaparte and Gross study) would be repaired under warrantee and would occur in the first few years of operation. Hence, any destruction costs incurred would be minimal and potentially paid by the landfill owner. Second, it is assumed that the landfill liner market is competitive. As a result, in order to secure the largest share of the market, the liner manufacturers would naturally offer their product at the most competitive price possible, and the product guarantee must be considered as part of the price consideration. Simply put, a manufacturer that could give a longer guarantee would be in a more advantageous market position and would not hesitate to do so; however, the length of the guarantees is consistent across manufacturers. As a result, this analysis will share the liner manufacturer's confidence in the 20-year liner life and use it as the age to landfill failure.

Given the strong influence of the time value of money in financial analysis and the uncertainty of the time to failure, rather than a single time when failure probability increased from 0 to 100 percent, a step function, a standard distribution of failure probabilities, was established. If a standard bell-shaped probability curve with a 95 percent confidence limit for failure between 20 and 25 years is used and expressed on a cumulative basis, the resulting failure probability distribution would be as shown in Fig. 4-7. This cumulative probability distribution leads

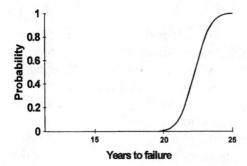

Figure 4-7. Probability of a new landfill failing.

logically to the concept of expected value, which when combined with present value calculations can be used to derive the
cost or liability factor for landfill failure.

Expressing the Expected Value of Landfill Failure

From the definition of expected value, probability of the event
times the cost-benefit of the event, half the needed information is
available; the probability of failure at any given time can be
directly calculated from the Fig. 4-7 distribution. However,
unlike in the example given previously where all probable
events would occur simultaneously, the probability of landfill
failure is spread over years. In present value terms, the financial
liability to the firm in any given year is a function of the expectation of failure, the discount rate used, and the cost of destruction.

In addition, since future costs must be discounted, the age of
the landfill when the waste is deposited is an important consideration. Given the estimated 20-year liner life, the present value
of the cost of failure would be considerably higher in a landfill
that was 17 years old (i.e., failure probability rising within 3
years) than it would be if the landfill were nearly new (i.e., failure probability rising in 20 years). As a result, the analysis lends
itself to a family of factors with each representing the expected
value of landfill failure at a specific landfill age.

Model Development

The critical aspect of applying microeconomic methods to predicting long-term landfill liability cost lies in the ability to predict the social cost (P_s in Fig. 4-6). Since the validity of using P_s to determine the total cost was established, all that remains is to predict its magnitude through combining the failure probability, expected value, and discount rate into a single function.

One more simplification was made in developing this model. Given that the present value equation is a method to express the value of a future expenditure in terms of present value, the future cost of waste destruction had to be estimated. With the specific intent of ensuring that the model not overestimate the savings that were possible by avoiding the generation of waste, it was assumed that the cost of waste destruction will be constant over time. Although this assumption may seem unlikely, it is based on microeconomic market theory. First, one must accept the fact that landfills are filling up and there is a maximum available volume. These facts should drive the price of landfilling hazardous waste toward the maximum, the price of waste destruction. The shrinking of the difference between landfill tipping fees and price of destruction technologies will create business opportunities for entrepreneurs who want to enter the destruction market. This change in the supply parameter of number of suppliers should drive the cost of destruction technology down enough to balance the causes of rising prices such as inflation. Hence, even though the price of landfilling waste (a competing technology) is predicted to rise, the net result of market forces on the unit price of waste destruction would be relative consistency. Again, unless one believes that the unit cost of destruction technologies will decrease, this assumption is either valid or conservative in that it will underestimate the magnitude of future destruction costs.

This assumption further means that because in the computations the future destruction cost is a constant, it can be normalized to $1.00 versus being computed for each separate destruction cost in future years.

When it comes to computing the expected value, this case is slightly more involved than that previously discussed. In computing the expected value of landfill failure, the fact that there are separate, distinct probabilities of the landfill failing in any given year, tends toward computational complexity, but the method is straightforward. For example, in the case of roulette discussed earlier, the expected value computation was simplified because each number on the wheel carried an equal probability of being selected. If the equation were written more accurately, it would be

$$\text{Expected value} = \frac{1}{38}(\$36.00) - \Sigma(P_i)(\text{value}_i)$$

Because the cost of failure is the same for each of the losing 37 numbers, the equation can be simplified to

$$\text{Expected value} = \frac{1}{38}(\$36.00) - \$1.00\left[\left(\frac{1}{37}\right) + \left(\frac{1}{37}\right)\cdots\right]$$

This can be further simplified to the equation shown in the previous section.

In analyzing the expected value of landfill failure, the above simplifications cannot be made because each year in the future carries both a distinct failure probability and, because of the time dependence in the calculation of present value, a distinct cost of failure. Hence, the expected value for each year must be computed separately. Then, because those values would represent the expected value, in present value terms, of the failure for each particular year, summing them over all the years would give the total expected value of failure.

To demonstrate the calculations, assume a firm is considering sending its waste to a new landfill. Hence, the cumulative probability graph shown earlier would be valid. If the firm used a 10 percent discount rate, the present value factors for a $1.00 investment could be computed using the present value equation. Then the products of the individual year's probabilities and present value factors could be added to show the total expected value, per dollar of destruction costs, for waste placed in that landfill. Table 4-4 shows these computations. The sum of the expected values, shown as the liability factor in Table 4-4, represents the fraction of destruction costs that the firm should consider in its financial analysis. Since there was a zero failure probability through year 20, the expected value in those years is

Table 4-4. Liability Factors for New Landfill (10 Percent Interest Compounded Annually)

Year	PV at 10 percent	Fail probability	Expected value
1	0.909090909	0	0
2	0.826446281	0	0
3	0.751314801	0	0
4	0.683013455	0	0
5	0.620921323	0	0
6	0.56447393	0	0
7	0.513158118	0	0
8	0.46650738	0	0
9	0.424097618	0	0
10	0.385543289	0	0
11	0.350493899	0	0
12	0.318630818	0	0
13	0.28966438	0	0
14	0.263331254	0	0
15	0.239392049	0	0
16	0.217629136	0	0
17	0.197844669	0	0
18	0.17985879	0	0
19	0.163507991	0	0
20	0.148643628	0	0
21	0.135130571	0.02	0.002703
22	0.122845974	0.14	0.017198
23	0.111678158	0.34	0.037971
24	0.101525598	0.34	0.034519
25	0.092295998	0.14	0.012921
26	0.083905453	0.02	0.001678
Liability factor			0.10699

Table 4-5. Liability Factors
(10 Percent Interest
Compounded Annually)

Year	Liability factor
1	0.107
2	0.118
3	0.129
4	0.142
5	0.157
6	0.172
7	0.19
8	0.209
9	0.229
10	0.252
11	0.278
12	0.305
13	0.336
14	0.369
15	0.406
16	0.445
17	0.492
18	0.541
19	0.595
20	0.654
21	0.72
22	0.79
23	0.854
24	0.894
25	0.907
26	0.909

likewise zero. Then, as the probability increases over the next 5 years, the expected value likewise changes. If the analyst felt that the probability should be spread over 10 years, the same computations would be made with different annual probabilities. Hence, this liability factor (f_L), when multiplied by the current cost of waste destruction, would represent the present value of the future destruction cost (i.e., P_s from Fig. 4-7—the social cost of disposing of the waste in the landfill.)

If these calculations were repeated for all other landfill ages from 0 through 26 years, the family of liability factors shown in Table 4-5 would result.

Similarly, these liability factors can be graphed as a single line as in Fig. 4.8. The line shows all the liability factors (f_L) for a 10 percent discount rate which represent the total percentage of the destruction cost that should be added to the landfill cost in financial analyses. This line need only be established a single time at the set interest rate for the firm. Then the liability factor can be read directly off the graph by entering from the horizontal axis at the age of the landfill being used or being considered, moving vertically up to the line established at the selected discount rate, and the expected value factor read off the vertical axis. The resultant factor, when multiplied by the cost of waste destruction, represents the present value of the future destruc-

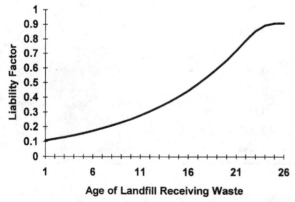

Figure 4-8. Liability factors with a 10 percent discount rate.

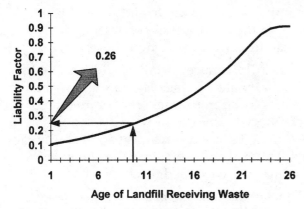

Figure 4-9. Example liability factor calculations.

tion cost (i.e., P_s, the social cost of disposing of the waste in the landfill.) For example, Figure 4-9 shows how the graph would be used if a landfill being considered for disposal is 9½ years old and the discount rate used by the firm is 10 percent.

The factor from the graph, 0.26, represents the fraction of the cost of destroying the waste that must be considered in the present value of landfilling the waste according to $P_t = P_1 + (f_L)P_d$. If the costs for landfilling and destruction were $100 and $300 per unit of waste, respectively, the total cost that the firm should use in calculating the cost of landfilling the waste would be $100 + (0.26)($300) = $178, which is 78 percent higher than would otherwise be recognized by the firm. In computing the benefit of a pollution prevention technology, it is this $178 that should be used in computing the benefit of not generating hazardous waste.

Conclusions

A number of assumptions were required both in developing the model and in simplifying its presentation for this text. The most significant assumptions and their potential impact on the liability factor are

Assumption 1.   Due to advances in landfill design, the key factor in determining future liability costs for landfills will be the ultimate destruction of the waste. This assumption ignores the costs of waste removal, transportation, and so on during the remediation; however, if incurred, these costs will add to the expense, making the liability factor prediction conservative.

Assumption 2.   Landfill "failure" shall be determined by restrictions on the maximum and average leachate flow from the landfill. If the EPA takes a different track in promulgating the upcoming RCRA reauthorization, the only effect would be to extend/contract the time to failure. In this case, the liability factor analysis outlined herein would remain valid; however, the time to landfill failure may have to be adjusted.

Assumption 3.   Destruction cost increases shall be balanced by cost decreases due to technological development yielding a constant unit cost for waste destruction. Although this is impossible to predict accurately, as with the effect of limiting the analysis to destruction costs, if the prices do increase, the net effect will be to underestimate the total long-term liability, again leading to the liability factor being conservative.

Assumption 4.   Inflation over the period was taken as zero. This was a simplification used only in the text example; however, given that any inflation rate in excess of zero would increase the costs of destruction, it leads to a conservative estimate of the present value cost of landfilling the waste. If a firm chose to include destruction cost increases in their calculations, the equation would be modified only slightly. Instead of computing the sum of all expected values for a $1.00 investment, the firm would calculate the actual expected values. For example, if the $300 per ton destruction costs were inflated at a moderate 3 percent rate, the computation for disposing of waste in a 10-year-old landfill would be as shown in Table 4-6.

As shown in the table, even with a relatively modest inflation rate, the actual cost of destruction at the time of failure would be over $400 per ton, and the resulting cost of landfilling a ton of waste which should be considered by the waste generator would be $224 (i.e., $100 + $124) versus $178. If a firm has specific inflation factors for use in financial analysis, they can be easily included in this model.

The key to this analysis was the use of the principles of microeconomics and engineering economics to predict the total cost of

Table 4-6. Expected Value Computations with Increasing Destruction Costs

Year	PV at 10 percent	Fail probability	Destruction cost	Expected value
1	0.909091	0	$309	$0
2	0.826446	0	318	0
3	0.751315	0	328	0
4	0.683013	0	338	0
5	0.620921	0	348	0
6	0.564474	0	358	0
7	0.513158	0	369	0
8	0.466507	0	380	0
9	0.424098	0	391	0
10	0.385543	0	403	0
11	0.350494	0.02	415	3
12	0.318631	0.14	428	19
13	0.289664	0.34	441	43
14	0.263331	0.34	454	41
15	0.239392	0.14	467	16
16	0.217629	0.02	481	2
17	0.197845		496	
18	0.179859		511	
19	0.163508		526	
20	0.148644		542	
21	0.135131		558	
22	0.122846		575	
23	0.111678		592	
24	0.101526		610	
25	0.092296		628	
26	0.083905		647	
Total expected value				$124

landfilling hazardous waste. As shown, the magnitude of the negative externality in landfilling hazardous waste (P_s) is a cost over and above the actual tipping fee (P_l). Hence, the total cost of landfilling waste was the actual cost of the landfill's tipping fee, considered by the waste producer, plus the cost of the pseudonegative externality such that $P_t = P_l + P_s$.

In terms of the liability factor, the total cost can also be written as $P_t = P_l + f_L P_d$. Combining these two equations leads to

$$P_t = P_l + P_s = P_l + f_L P_d$$

In other words, given a constant price for waste destruction, the negative externality is equivalent to the liability factor prediction, or

$$P_s = f_L P_d$$

The importance of this equation is that the prediction of the social cost becomes independent of the landfill cost. Further, there are no limitations on the destruction cost variable. It can be the cost of any form of waste destruction, relocating waste at remediation to a different landfill, or even a pollution prevention technology. The only variable of concern is that of inflation. Given that most firms or individuals involved in business either have set guidelines or personal estimation techniques, predicting inflation can be left up to the investor.

Such analyses, based in sound microeconomic and financial theory, provide a number of advantages. First, they eliminate having to deal with the technical problems of site inconsistencies which occur when applying costs estimated or known at one site to another, as currently practiced in liability estimation. Second, there is little doubt that the liability factor is conservative in that it could underestimate the total financial liability that a waste generator will ultimately face; however, this does not detract from the model's value. On the contrary, because of its conservative nature, even though the result can be a more than doubling of the tipping fee, there can be little technical or financial argument against using it in financial analysis. Third, because the factor was developed on a per-unit basis, there is no problem with economies of scale that is common in many business dealings. Finally, the liability factor eliminates potential problems in regional cost variation and price differences due to the firm's ability to negotiate with the landfill owner.

Although not the final answer to the problem of predicting future liability, the development of the liability factor demonstrates how the individual elements presented in the text can be combined to make a cost prediction which more accurately reflects the realities of waste disposal. Such models provide pollution prevention investors with elegant, simple tools to use in their fight for a firm's limited resources and a valuable lever to force pollution prevention.

Study Concepts

1. Given competing technologies, be able to rank them on the pollution prevention hierarchy contained in the Pollution Prevention Act, as presented by Baker, or as explained in the text to determine the "best" option.

2. Be able to discuss the difference between waste reduction, such as required under RCRA, and "true" pollution prevention as required by the Pollution Prevention Act of 1990.

3. Be able to discuss the difficulties in expressing pollution prevention by measuring the quantities of hazardous waste generated.

4. Be able to discuss various data sources which would apply to determining investment alternatives.

5. Be able to discuss how indexing and throughput ratio would be used either to predict future hazardous waste generation or to examine the results of previous pollution prevention investments.

6. Be able to discuss the limitations involved in using prediction and/or measurement techniques such as indexing.

7. Be able to discuss the role that toxicity and the receiving medium play in determining investment alternatives.

5
Some Last Thoughts

*Preventing pollution is a far more
efficient strategy than struggling to deal
with the problems once they've occurred.
. . . It's time to reorient ourselves, using
technologies and processes that reduce or
prevent pollution, to stop it before it
starts.* PRESIDENT GEORGE BUSH
June 8, 1989

The goal of this text has been to provide methods and tools
rather than answers. Given the ever-increasing number of environmental requirements and the nearly endless number of technical solutions to problems, it is impossible for any single text to
cover all possible pollution prevention investment opportunities. Instead, this text is intended as an advanced primer for
environmental managers. As shown in the appendix, the understanding of the basics of microeconomics, engineering economics, and accounting make even complex issues relatively easy to
understand and analyze—analyses that can be used to justify
pollution prevention investment.

If firms are to advance on both environmental and economic fronts, there are two choices; either financial management personnel must be taught environmental engineering and management, or the environmental engineers and managers must be taught financial management. It is the latter option that has been chosen in this text. By learning the basic tools and language of financial management, environmental personnel will be in a position to fight for resources within firms or from financial institutions.

It has been said that we do not inherit the earth from our parents—instead, we borrow it from our children. To judge how we are doing, one only has to turn on the television or pick up a newspaper to hear the pundits and "doom-and-gloom" prophets telling us what a mess we are in and what we need to do to save our planet. Conversely, an equal number of pundits are citing the improvements in water and air quality that have been made which imply that we have are making good headway in dealing with our environmental problems. With all the differing opinions, it is little wonder that environmental programs sometimes seem to be going in circles.

Pollution prevention can be a major factor in organizing our attack and giving direction to an overall approach to environmental improvement. While it has not yet been decided which approach will be taken in regulating industry's efforts in pollution prevention, there is little doubt that the focus of environmental regulation will move away from waste treatment and toward waste avoidance. It is within these bounds that pollution prevention can find its most ardent supporters. Not only will pollution prevention satisfy critics such as Dr. S. Fred Singer (1984) of the National Advisory Committee on Oceans and Atmosphere in "Acid Rain: A Billion Dollar Solution to a Million Dollar Problem" who feel we have gone too far, but, for those who think we are doing too little, how can they say that not generating pollution is bad?

Perhaps the article written by James Speth, Russell Train, and Douglas Costle (1992) best explains this concept. These individuals held positions which allowed them to direct national policy in this country—two were EPA administrators and the other a science advisor—during the peak of the command-and-control regulatory approach. Their message to current and future regulators is clear:

> Despite recurring conflicts on the environment-economy front, few Americans really want to sacrifice one for the other. . . . Unfortunately, current approaches won't get us there. What's needed is a new national strategy that fuses the goals of a healthy environment and a strong economy, advancing both causes simultaneously.
>
> The good news is that such win-win policies do exist. . . . Environmental demands will create major economic opportunities, and nations and companies that see these opportunities and seize them can capture an early share of growing markets. Ambitious environmental laws—at least those that promote innovation and efficient, cost-effective approaches—can thus help provide a competitive edge. . . .
>
> The problem is that the current U.S. approach to environmental protection, a product of the early 1970s, is no match for the environmental and economic challenges we now face. Now we rely on a command and control system of regulation with adversarial relations among industry, regulators and environmentalists. This system focuses on cleaning up pollution at the end of the pipe or the top of the smokestack, neglecting the need to consider product design production process, and environmental factors together.
>
> While the current approach has accomplished a great deal—the air in our cities is markedly cleaner than it was two decades ago—it has peaked in effectiveness. Our system of environmental regulation is ill-suited to emerging global-scale problems. It is also inhibiting innovation and least-cost solutions that could strengthen U.S. economic performance.
>
> For all these reasons, a new paradigm is needed for environmental governance in the United States—one reflecting a basic shift in emphasis from restrictions to incentives and from reacting after the fact to anticipating future needs and opportunities. As it proves itself, this new model should replace the old, which can be held in reserve for scofflaws and laggards.

When the people who were instrumental in establishing the command-and-control approach to solving environmental problems say it's time to change, perhaps it's time someone listened. The key to the change is economics. All the key elements brought out by Speth, Train, and Costle are contained within this concept: What would be a stronger incentive for a company to invest in pollution prevention than the desire to increase profit (pollution prevention pays)? What would be a better incentive for environmental activist who think we are doing too little than to provide a cleaner environment (pollution prevention eliminates or reduces pollution)? Finally, what would serve as a greater inducement or provide a larger benefit to the consumer than to improve the environment while making goods available at lower costs (pollution prevention is driven by lower costs)? Clearly, if proper financial justification is provided, pollution prevention is a win-win-win situation.

References and Additional Readings

Ackerman, D. G., Jr., and Venezia, R. A. "Oceanic Incineration," in Freeman, Harry M., ed., *Standard Handbook of Hazardous Waste Treatment and Disposal*, New York, McGraw-Hill, 1989.

Aldrich, J. R. *A Practical Guide to Justifying Pollution Prevention Projects*, American Institute of Pollution Prevention, 1992.

Bach, G. L. *Micro-Economics, Analysis and Applications*, Englewood Cliffs, N.J., Prentice-Hall, 1980.

Baker, R. D., Dunforn, R. W., and Warren, J. L. *Alternatives for Measuring Hazardous Waste Reduction*, Hazardous Waste Research and Information Center, HWRIC RR-056, April 1991.

Baumol, W. J., and Oates, W. E. *The Theory of Environmental Policy*, 2d ed., Cambridge, England, Cambridge University Press, 1988.

Bonaparte, A. M., and Gross, A. M. "Field Behavior of Double-Liner Systems," *Waste Containment Systems: Construction, Regulation, and Performance*, Geotechnical Special Publication no. 26, New York, American Society of Civil Engineers, November 1990.

Butler, D., Timm, C. M., and Fromm, C. *Justification of Waste Reduction Projects by Comprehensive Cost-Benefit Analysis*, Jacobs Engineering Group Inc., undated.

Carlson, K. L., and Burnett, C. *Hazardous Waste Minimization Project Economic Assessment*, HAZMAT Conference, Atlantic City, N.J., June 3, 1986.

Comprehensive Environmental Response, Compensation and Liability Act (CERCLA), secs. 106, 107(a–b).

Cornes, R., and Saddler, T. *The Theory of Externalities, Public Goods, and Club Goods*, New York, Cambridge University Press, 1986.

Daniel, D. E., et al. *Rate of Flow of Leachate through Clay Soil Liners*, US EPA, EPA/600/SD-91/021, July 1991.

Davidson, S., Stickney, C. P., and Weil, R. L. *Financial Accounting: An Introduction to Concepts, Methods, and Uses,* 5th ed., Chicago, Harcourt Brace Jovanovich, 1988.

Evans, G. M. "Cost Perspectives for Hazardous-Waste Management," in Freeman, Harry M., ed., *Standard Handbook of Hazardous Waste Treatment and Disposal,* New York, McGraw-Hill, 1989.

Freeman, A. M. *Air and Water Pollution Control: A Benefit-Cost Assessment,* New York, Wiley, 1982a.

Freeman A. M. *The Benefits of Environmental Improvement,* New York, Wiley, 1982b, pp. 38–50.

Fribush, S. L. *Economics Research for Waste Minimization,* Presentation at Engineering Foundation Conference on Engineering to Minimize the Generation of Hazardous Waste, New Hampshire, July 29, 1987.

Fromm, C. H., and Butler, D. *Practical Guidelines for Estimating the Profitability of Waste Minimization Measures,* HAZMAT Conference, Atlantic City, N.J., June 3, 1986.

Hartwick, J. M., and Olewiler, N. *The Economics of Natural Resource Use,* New York, Harper and Row, 1986.

Hazardous Materials Technical Center, Washington, D.C., vol. 8, no. 5, September 1989.

Hazardous Waste News, April 23, 1990.

Hazardous Waste News, May 28, 1990.

Hovater, L. R. "Synthetic Linings," in Freeman, H. M., ed., *Standard Handbook of Hazardous Waste Treatment and Disposal,* New York, McGraw-Hill, 1989, p. 10.31.

Incentives and Barriers to Commercializing Environmental Technologies, University of Pittsburgh Applied Research Center, March 1990.

Just, R. E., Hueth, D. L., and Schmitz, A. *Applied Welfare Economics and Public Policy,* Englewood Cliffs, N.J., Prentice-Hall, 1982.

Leu, D. J., Wilhelm, K., and Low, J. *State Economic and Regulatory Incentives for Waste Minimization,* Alternative Technology Section, California Department of Health Services, Sacramento, 1986.

MacLean, R. W. *Estimating Future Liability Costs for Waste Management Options,* Hazardous and Solid Waste Conference, Washington, D.C., November 19–20, 1987a.

MacLean, R. W. *Financial Analysis of Waste Management Alternatives,* General Electric Corporate Environmental Programs, Fairfield, Conn., 1987b.

MacLean, R. W. *Motivating Industry toward Waste Minimization and Clean Technology,* ISWA and EPA Conference, Geneva, Switzerland, May 30, 1989.

Mansfield, E. *Microeconomics: Theory and Applications*, New York, Norton, 1988.

McHugh, R. T. "The Economics of Waste Minimization," in Freeman, H. M., ed., *Hazardous Waste Minimization*, New York, McGraw-Hill, 1990, p. 132.

Mills, E. S., and Graves, P. E. *The Economics of Environmental Quality*, 2d ed., New York, Norton, 1986, p. 105.

Morey, E. "Confuser Surplus," *American Economic Review*, vol. 74, no. 1, March 1984, pp. 163–173.

Pearce, D. W., and Turner, R. K. *Economics of Natural Resources and the Environment*, Baltimore, Johns Hopkins University Press, 1990.

Pindyck, R. S., and Rubinfeld, D. L. *Microeconomics*, New York, MacMillan, 1989.

Purcell, A. *The "Economic Imperative,"* Government Institutes, Inc., 1985.

Resource Conservation and Recovery Act, Subtitle C, Section 3001.

Rosner, B. *Fundamentals of Biostatistics*, Boston, PWS-Kent Publishing, 1986.

Seneca, J. J., and Taussig, M. K. *Environmental Economics*, Englewood Cliffs, N.J., Prentice-Hall, 1974.

Singer, S. Fred. "Acid Rain: A Billion Dollar Solution to a Million Dollar Problem," *Policy Review*, no. 27, Winter 1984.

Speth, J. G., Train, R. E., and Costle, D. M. "Double or Nothing: Linking U.S. Economic and Environmental Objectives," *WRI Issues and Ideas*, World Resources Institute, November 1992.

Tietenberg, T. H. *Emissions Trading*, Washington, D.C., Resources for the Future, 1985.

Tietenberg, T. H. *Environmental and Natural Resource Economics*, Washington, D.C., Resources for the Future, 1987.

U.S. Environmental Protection Agency. Method 9090, "Liner Compatibility Test," US EPA Office of Solid Waste, *Federal Register*, vol. 49, no. 191, October 1, 1984.

U.S. Environmental Protection Agency. *Pollution Prevention Benefits Manual*, US EPA Office of Solid Waste and Office of Policy, Planning and Evaluation, ICF Inc., December 1988.

US EPA Letter, November 27, 1990, *Pollution Prevention Act of 1990*, from Director of Office of Pollution Prevention.

Willig, R. "Consumer's Surplus without Apology," *American Economic Review*, vol. 66, September 1976, pp. 589–597.

Index

About the Author

James R. Aldrich, Ph.D., is the single point of contact for the Turkish General Staff in the Office of Defense Cooperation, Turkey, where he is responsible for a number of programs, including engineering and construction in-country, bilateral agreements, and environmental matters. He also teaches hazardous waste management courses at the Middle East Technical University in Ankara, Turkey. He was formerly assistance professor of environmental engineering at the Air Force Institute of Technology in Ohio. Major Aldrich is the recipient of many awards, including the 1984 Air Force Environmental Engineer of the Year Award, and is principal author of *A Primer for Financial Analysis of Pollution Prevention Projects*. He holds several patents, and is also the author of numerous articles and studies.

DATE